Pork Chops and Applesauce

A Collection of Recipes and Reflections

By

Cynthia Briggs

ISBN: 1-4033-8164-X (e-book)
ISBN: 1-4033-8165-8 (Paperback)
ISBN: 1-4033-8166-6 (Hardcover)

Library of Congress Control Number: 2002094903

This book is printed on acid free paper.

Printed in the United States of America
Bloomington, IN

1stBooks – rev. 06/16/04

Dedication

To my husband, Ed, you had unwavering confidence in me that *Pork Chops & Applesauce, A Collection of Recipes and Reflections* would come to fruition. You understood the depth of my passions for cooking and writing; and you believed that my passions, combined with my perseverance and my appreciation of the subtle humor in everyday life, were a winning combination to publication.

Thank you, Sweetheart, for your patience and love, even in the face of chaos at deadline time; and for trusting that I would eventually return to the kitchen!

First, to my friend, and second, to my creative editor, Denise von Pressentin, we did it! Our vow to honor our friendship first and foremost above the demands of getting *Pork Chops & Applesauce* to print was done with the utmost of ease.

Thank you, dear friend, for sharing your creative energy, and your generous, uplifting support. Your margin notations, "This is good imagery!" or "I love this sentence!" were often the encouraging comments that kept me going.

To my mom, Betty Belles, your many recipes, cooking advice and flavorful stories, provided the backbone to *Pork Chops & Applesauce,* and added to its tender hearth and home character.

Thank you, Mom, for teaching me how to become a master in my own kitchen and for honoring the memory of days gone by as sterling reflections of my heritage.

To my children, Holly and Brian Robertson, your childhood antics stocked my story larder full of tales to tell - and books to write.

Thank you both for just being yourselves, and for giving me five terrific grandchildren!

To my aunt, Joy Pape, for your advice, "Do not cut *anything* out of your story, the details are what gives it heart."

Thank you, Aunt Joy, for believing in my writing talent long before I got down to the real business of putting pen to paper.

Thank you to family, friends and well-wishers for sharing your heartwarming tales and cherished recipes as they are the silver threads-of-life, which make up the fabric of *Pork Chops & Applesauce, A Collection of Recipes and Reflections*.

Many thanks to those who generously granted written permission for me to reprint their recipes.

To my father,
Robert Belles,
your memory continues
to shape who I am today.

Introduction

"Your bull, Snoopy, has jumped the fence again and he's looking for our heifer," was a frequent, and often frantic, telephone call I'd receive from my neighbor back in the 1970s. Often, the phone call would take me away from a hot kitchen stove where I was preserving dozens of quarts of steamy applesauce.

Sometimes as I was chasing our runaway weaner pigs through the rear of our 3-acre spread, my neighbor would call to me from his dairy barn to apprise me of Snoopy's most recent escapade. During those hectic and harried years I'd often ask myself, "What's my purpose here?"

I knew the answer to the question. I wanted my 2 children to experience the wholesome advantages of being raised on a farm. But sometimes I questioned whether it was really worth all the hard work when I returned home spent from chasing our escaped livestock back home from neighboring farms.

Thirty years later, when I started putting pen to paper for a rural community newspaper near Seattle, my purpose as a farm Mom took on new meaning. Unknowingly, I'd spent those years stocking my story larder - I'd been storing fodder for a cooking column to be written in the 90s followed by a collection of recipes and reflections.

Like a robin building her spring nest, I had been gathering dry twigs and stray pieces of yarn, weaving together the nest fibers of my life. Through my cooking column I began recalling the many humorous events that stemmed from raising my children in the country and re-living my own memorable adventures as a farm kid growing up in the 50s near my grandparent's farm in eastern Oregon.

In creating this book, I spent 4 years writing and cooking, cooking and writing; immersing myself in my two most loved creative efforts. I began looking at food and cooking as more than just eating or making a meal, but as a link that connected people of all origins and backgrounds. Through the acts of harvesting, preserving, and cooking food, relationships are frequently strengthened, or doors often swing open to welcome new opportunities for friendships. Food and cooking remain the fine threads, which weave families and friends more tightly together.

When reflecting upon our past, generally food serves as a backdrop to our celebratory occasions – we don't usually meet simply to eat – we gather to celebrate, bond and support others and sharing food is a gesture of our sincerity. Food is synonymous with our traditional and religious ceremonies, and our holidays - it's even important at our tailgate parties. It's difficult to think of an occasion where we don't break bread with family, friends or acquaintances.

Food is symbolic of what we've done in our lives; it's part of our history. I learned about kneading whole-wheat bread when we visited Grandma's house at Thanksgiving. Tossing together a Caesar salad from memory was something my gray-haired neighbor, Mrs. Mattson, taught me when I was 14. And the sweet remembrance of sitting in Aunt M's bright yellow breakfast nook, overlooking the duck pond, and gobbling down a warm-from-the-oven gooey sticky-bun is as vivid today as it was 40 years ago.

Because I've long been intrigued with our food and cooking connections with friends and family, it is essential for me in my writing that each story has a heart-point. By that I mean a sentence or a phrase that triggers a memory in the reader's heart, which connects to the heart of my story – creating a heart-point.

You're invited to join me in opening your story larder of remembrances as you read *Pork Chops & Applesauce - A Collection of Recipes and Reflections* a cookbook that I planted, cultivated and harvested from my heart.

Homemade Chunky Applesauce

6 to 8 apples, peeled, cored, diced
¼ cup water
1 heaping teaspoon ground cinnamon
½ teaspoon ground cardamom
¼ teaspoon ground nutmeg
½ cup granulated sugar

Place prepared apples in a large saucepan, add water, cinnamon, cardamom, nutmeg and sugar. Stir slightly to blend spices, cover with a tight-fitting lid. Place over medium heat. When apples begin to steam, turn heat to low. Simmer for 20-30 minutes, stirring occasionally to avoid scorching. When apples are tender, remove from heat and mash with a hand-held potato masher. Serve warm with baked, pan-fried or grilled pork chops.
Makes 6 cups applesauce.

Homemade Pork Chops

6 – 1 inch thick, bone- in pork chops
3 tablespoons cooking oil
Salt, pepper and garlic powder to taste

Treat a heavy skillet with non-stick cooking spray, place skillet over medium-high heat. When skillet begins to heat up, sprinkle garlic powder, salt and pepper in bottom of pan, add cooking oil to cover bottom of pan. When dimples begin to appear in the oil, add chops and pan-fry over medium heat for 10 minutes on each side, or until chops are crispy and brown on the outside with no visible pink inside next to the bone. Serve with warm homemade chunky applesauce. Makes 6 servings

Table of Contents

*We remember with fondness the folks
with whom we share our daily meals.*

Chapter One

Starters, Side Dishes and Specialties

What child hasn't set-up at least one lemonade stand during his or her long and lazy sultry summer vacation? It's something I remember doing as a child, although I do not recall luring quite as many "customers" as my kids managed to do from their road-side corner stand at the entrance of our 3-acre farm in Washington State.

Chapter one is a selection of starters, side dishes and specialties, all of which I've served my guests - starting with frosty lemonade to keep sweltering afternoons at bay, to ham and fresh-picked asparagus roll-ups in the springtime, and tempting make-ahead cheese balls presented during the chilly months on my holiday buffet table.

Whatever the season, I think you'll find something in this opening chapter that will tantalize your culinary talents and make your "taster" stand up and take notice.

CB

Cooling off in the Dog Days of Summer

"We're building a lemonade stand!" Brian announced excitedly as he power-walked through the kitchen looking for white butcher's paper. "May we borrow two bamboo poles from under the string bean bushes?" He didn't wait for my answer as the screen door slammed behind him.

The Pacific Northwest was experiencing a rare August heat wave, something that my two webbed-footed children, Brian and Holly, were experiencing for the first time at the tender ages of 4 and 6, respectively. The kids had been loafing around all summer complaining, "we don't have anything to do," and now that a heat spell had blanketed the area they feared they were "going to sweat to death!"

Trying to soothe their woes, I stirred up some fresh lemonade and suggested they go outside and sit under the shade of our Italian plum tree to drink it. "Before you know it, you'll be cooled off." I assured them.

As soon as their tumblers of lemonade were emptied, the kids scrambled to their feet and started gathering materials to build their first lemonade stand.

I smiled to myself thinking how the citrus refreshment I'd served them spurred their imaginations and how fast the old fashioned drink revived their spirits. The magic juice of summer had turned my whining, lethargic children into dynamos of activity with no mention of the wilting heat.

Comments from the kids like, "melting into a puddle under the hot sun" and "bored out of our gourds" suddenly evaporated into dog-day summer phrases of the past. I mixed up a generous pitcher of cold lemonade anticipating that the kids would soon be begging me to make the sweet-tart beverage to serve their customers. From the living room window I could see my sunburned urchins sitting behind their storefront, which they'd constructed by tying dilapidated wooden orange crates together with green garden jute. "*LEMONADE 10¢*" was scrawled across a butcher paper sign supported by two bamboo beanpoles that wafted precariously in the sultry summer breeze.

The kids' first customer of the day drove up in a shiny black Ford Taurus. I was amused to see a tall slender man in a business suit digging in his pockets for change. Hurriedly, he walked toward the stand, and took the brimming-over-the-top paper cup the kids had eagerly filled with lemonade. The man eagerly gulped it down. Before he went on his way, he flashed the kids a satisfied smile, as if to say, "That hit the spot!"

Near the end of the afternoon, I looked up to see two joggers taking a break near the makeshift refreshment bar. They were guzzling down "tall cool ones" as though they were rarified elixirs of life.

The neighborhood kids stopped by to say "Hi!" on their way back from the lake and agreeably chug-a-lugged the last three cups of frosty brew. Holly and Brian closed-up for the day.

My young entrepreneurs earned over $3 that day selling lemonade. But far more important than the money was the lesson they learned. They provided a service that met the needs of wilting passersby. It seemed that folks couldn't resist stopping to buy lemonade from two dirty-faced children who manned their self-built roadside stand.

As the sun touched the horizon that evening and filled the sky with a blazing red sunset, I asked myself, "were people paying 10 cents for a glass of lemonade, or were they purchasing a glimpse into their pasts?" I feel they were buying a brief respite, which brought back memories of their own youthful summertime experiences and how they, too, might have learned, "when life gives you lemons…make lemonade!"

State Fair Lemonade

10 lemons
1 cup granulated sugar
10 ice cubes
Cold water

Wash lemons and bring them to room temperature. Roll lemons on a firm surface, slice in half and squeeze into gallon container. Pick out and discard any visible seeds. Toss lemon rinds into container. Pour sugar over rinds and let mixture sit for ½ hour. Add ice cubes and enough water to fill container. Stir thoroughly and serve over additional ice cubes. Garnish with fresh mint, if desired. Makes 6-8 serving.

"Something for the Adults" Lemonade

Juice of 2 lemons
Juice of 2 limes
6 heaping tablespoons confectioners' sugar
2 teaspoons Grenadine
3 ounces light rum or vodka (optional)
Carbonated water
3 orange slices
3 lemon slices
3 maraschino cherries
Fresh mint leaves

Shake vodka, lime and lemon juices, sugar and Grenadine with ice and strain into Collins glasses over shaved ice. Fill glass with carbonated water and stir. Splash top with a dash of Maraschino cherry juice, decorate with orange and lemon slices; add a sprig of mint and a cherry. Serve with a straw. Makes 3 servings.

Search for Wild Asparagus Spans Generations

I was only 5 years old when I first went asparagus hunting with my mom and dad on the sandy riverbanks of the Columbia River in Eastern Oregon. The little "green pencil" sprouts seemed to tease me by poking their heads out from beneath the damp soil, always peeking out where I'd least expect to find them, much like playing hide and seek. Tirelessly, I scoured the shores hoping to discover green dotted asparagus patches.

In the years to come, I looked forward to our yearly asparagus excursions with a mixed feeling of excitement and anxiety. You see my mother instilled in me the terror of coming nose to nose with snakes that might have taken a notion to sun themselves on the warm, damp dunes. Yet, being allowed the privilege of wielding a machete, which was used for cutting the dark green shoots, boosted my young ego and quelled my terror. There were moments when I was so full of myself that I forget about the snakes that lurked in grassy mounds..."waiting to eat little girls!" I soon began anticipating spring when we'd go searching for the odd looking green vegetable that seemed to miraculously pop up from beneath the cream-colored sand.

History repeated itself in the mid 1970s when I found myself telling my young children, "Gramma & Grandpa used to bring me here every spring to cut asparagus. Just be sure to wear your boots and watch out for snakes!"

The kids eagerly embraced the springtime jaunts. At young ages they learned to pull on their boots and scout the gritty, musty coves seeking the stocky "green pencils" just as I had done as a child. However, some things had changed in 30 years. For instance, my kids couldn't be trusted with machetes for fear of what they might do to each other, and the feasibility of dodging rattlers between asparagus stalks was something they said, "only happened in the movies!"

Industrial progress and increased population had begun taking its toll on the area, invading the natural habitat of the wild asparagus. Fortunately, I was able to take my children on asparagus hunting adventures for a few years before I gave in to the reality of the disappearing growing areas. Urbanization did not reverse itself nor did the age-old reaction children often exhibit to eating the peculiar green branch.

"Yuck! Do I have to eat this stuff?" I remember saying to my parents when I first saw ready-to-eat, steaming asparagus stalks on my dinner plate. Thirty years later the same words echoed around my dining room when I served them to my children. As a child it was fun seeking the elusive green stalks on the riverbanks, but eating them was quite another story.

Eventually, I stopped saying "yuck!" when the asparagus sprigs were set before me, and started saying, "Mm, may I please have another helping?" as I'd developed an appreciation for their unique, delicate flavor and their interesting texture.

My childhood association with asparagus provided me with opportunities to experiment with different ways to prepare them. And, after packing nearly 100 pounds of asparagus into my freezer every year, I discovered that the wonderful, natural flavor of the odd looking green vegetable is enhanced when they are simply blanched and served chilled. Blanching or steaming asparagus is quick and easy, always elegant in presentation, and absolutely delicious.

I'm sharing with you my simple methods of steaming and blanching asparagus, along with my great summertime recipes for asparagus salad and asparagus cheese ham roll-ups.

Is it the wonderfully unique taste of sprightly asparagus sprouts that teases my palate? Perhaps that's partially why I have such an affinity for asparagus, but I think the main reason is because every year when those familiar "green pencils" appear in the produce department, I long to rush home to sharpen my machete and pull on my high-top boots!

Asparagus Cheese Ham Roll-ups

1 pound or 20 slices honey deli ham, sliced for rolling
1 pound or 20 slices provolone cheese, sliced for rolling
20 stalks asparagus, **blanched** and chilled (see directions below)
¼ - ½ cup mayonnaise
Fresh ground pepper
20 colored toothpicks

Allow cheese to sit at room temperature for 30 minutes before assembling roll-ups. Lay 10 slices of ham on a large work surface. Place one slice of cheese on each slice of ham, add 1 stalk of asparagus (lay it to one side of the ham/cheese slice for easier rolling), spread with 1 teaspoon mayonnaise, add a dash of freshly ground pepper. Roll up beginning with the asparagus side (not too tight) and secure with a toothpick.

Repeat process except begin with cheese slices, adding the ham. This alternates the outside color of the roll-ups. Makes 20 roll-ups.

Cynthia's Chilled Asparagus Salad

4 cups asparagus, cut into 1½" pieces, **blanched** and chilled (see directions below)
8 lettuce leaves
Blue cheese dressing or ranch dressing

Line 8 small, salad dishes with leaf lettuce, place ½ cup chilled asparagus on lettuce, serve with ranch or blue cheese dressing on the side. Ranch dressing is usually the more popular choice. Makes 8 servings.

Simply Elegant Steamed Asparagus

4 cups fresh asparagus, cut into 1½" pieces or 24
    stalks asparagus
½ teaspoon dried dill weed
1 tablespoons lemon juice
2 tablespoons butter, softened
Salt and freshly ground pepper to taste

Place asparagus in steamer basket and sprinkle with dill weed. Cover and steam for 14-16 minutes or until tender. Remove to a mixing bowl; and sprinkle with lemon juice, butter, salt and pepper. Toss and serve immediately. Makes 8 servings.

Blanching (Scalding) Vegetables

All vegetables, except green peppers, must be blanched before freezing. This scalding prevents undesirable changes in flavor. Blanching is done in either boiling water or steam. The boiling water method is usually more convenient for home use.

Time for blanching varies with each vegetable (asparagus: wash; cut into desired length; blanch **2 minutes** for thin stalks or **4 minutes** for thicker stalks). Use a large kettle with a lid. Put at least one gallon of water in the kettle and blanch only one-pound (about 1 quart) prepared asparagus at a time. Put the asparagus in a perforated metal basket or cheesecloth bag. When water in kettle is at a **good rolling boil**, immerse the asparagus. Put lid on kettle and begin to count time immediately. Keep heat high and kettle covered until blanching time is up. The same water can be used again but **be sure** to bring it back to a rolling boil before adding more asparagus.

Cool asparagus immediately in ice water. When thoroughly cold (about 5 to 10 minutes), drain and either use for desired recipe or pack for freezing. For freezing, pack asparagus firm, but not tight, in freezer container to within ½ inch of top. Do not add salt or other seasoning. Secure with lid and freeze at once.

Modified instructions for blanching asparagus taken from: *Kerr Home Canning Book and How to Freeze Foods*, Freezing Vegetables, 1972, page 46.

Call your local county extension service for more information about home canning and freezing.

Recipes can Reveal more than how to Prepare a Dish

Yesterday I said to a friend, "I have three vices: coffee, the television show, *Law & Order,* and recipes - reading, sharing, and collecting them." We laughed about the seriousness of my vices. But later I thought about how important cookbooks and good recipes are to those of us who love to cook. For me, there's a deeper meaning to collecting and sharing recipes than simply the number of cookbooks that sit on my kitchen shelf. Trading recipes is an effective and meaningful way for cooks to communicate, connect, and bond.

I've always taken it as a compliment when someone asks me for a recipe. I willingly share the recipe with the requestor even if I've just met the person for the first time. This often is a way to break the ice or "lend a cup of sugar" to a new acquaintance, and gets a relationship off to a good start. The person asking for the recipe has said, in essence, "I think you're creative. Our culinary interests are similar. We have something in common – food and cooking." At this point, the door swings open creating the potential for a blossoming friendship.

My cookbooks are dog-eared to the point that sometimes it's hard to decipher the titles or measurements required in the recipes. Grease has penetrated through several layers of pages and frequently I have to scrape cookie dough off the paper to read what size pan or baking temperature is needed. However, to me stains and sticky spots record my history in the kitchen along with each person who has sat at my dining room table.

I've kept two recipe folders that are precious to me. One folder is boldly marked "Mom B." which is stuffed with copies of recipes my mother has collected. The folder labeled "Mom W."

is a collection of original recipes that my husband's mother gave to me the last time we visited her.

I frequently take a nostalgic trip through our mothers' close-to-vintage recipes; reading through the worn slips of paper I'm inspired to make fluffy white meringue for my cream pies or to stir up a scratch-batch of old-fashion baked beans. I've learned the key ingredients that my mom puts in her famous goulash, and how she made that green Jell-O mold that wiggled on my dinner plate when I was 8 years old. My curiosity has piqued when I re-discover a recipe card that's falling apart from age and written in Swedish - then my interest suddenly plummets when I realize it's Mom W's recipe for lutefisk!

My recipe cards are folded, torn, and stapled. In general, many of my recipes have been hurriedly torn from magazines and scrawled on the back of envelopes. My overstuffed recipe boxes, tattered PTA cookbooks with notations in the margins, and overflowing, awkward shaped file folders are, in reality, a meticulously organized record of special individuals who have shared a part of their cooking creativity and history with me.

Recently, I came across a recipe for marinated garbanzo beans that my grandmother tore from a can of beans 30 years ago. Another recipe, Baked Broccoli and Cheese Side Dish, brought back memories; it was hand-written on green steno paper by my daughter, Holly, who brought the recipe home to me 20 years ago when she was only 12 – I treasure it! Both of these recipes were given to me with heartfelt meaning, and so every time I see that torn can label or the folded steno paper in my recipe box my heart re-connects with Gramma and Holly.

There is no generation gap when it comes to the endless sharing of food ideas and food combinations. In fact, recipes help us weave the threads that bond us closely together and they can assist in mending a threadbare relationship. I enjoy reading recipes because they allow me to revisit my past and connect with people that have touched my heart.

Baked Broccoli and Cheese Side Dish

½ cup onion, chopped
4 tablespoons butter or margarine
½ teaspoon salt
¼ cup flour
3 eggs, slightly beaten
2 -10 ounce packages chopped frozen broccoli
OR 2 -10 ounce packages chopped frozen spinach
1 - 5 ounce jar Kraft Old English Cheese
1 cup Nabisco Cheese Nips, crushed fine
4 teaspoons butter or margarine

Sauté onion in 4 tablespoons margarine until onions begin to soften. Stir in salt and flour. Fold in broccoli (or spinach), eggs and cheese. Spoon into 2-quart baking dish that has been coated with non-fat cooking spray. Sprinkle with crushed Cheese Nip crackers. Dot with 4 teaspoons margarine. Bake, uncovered, at 350° for 30 minutes. Makes 6 servings.

Beans, beans...the Perfect Recipe for a Family Reunion

We were clipping past lush green potato fields, and orderly rows of sugar beets, which sprawled as far as the eyes could see, as well as vast acres of low-growing fresh mint bordering Interstate 90. It was a sweltering August day in 1998. Ed and I had left Seattle before dawn and the first rooster crowing, so we could attend my Belles family reunion in Spokane, Washington.

Although Ed and I weren't married yet, I'd invited him to the reunion because it was the perfect opportunity for him to meet all my relatives. Ed had expressed his desire to marry me and I had agreed to marry him. But, one question remained - when? I really wanted to give him a resounding "yes!" but I was terrified of taking the plunge, and I'd been putting him off by using the excuse that we needed to wait, "until we've known each other longer."

"Did you know, dear, that Spokane is a mere 19 miles from Coeur d' Alene, Idaho?" Ed asked me with a slow, exceedingly deliberate wink. "What do you think?"

"And, just what are you hinting at Mr. Briggs?" I replied, holding back a smile and peering at him sideways through my sunglasses. Unlike Washington, which has a 3-day waiting period to get a marriage license, Idaho couples can get married within a matter of hours simply by relinquishing a few drops of blood and walking across the street to a justice of the peace.

"Maybe *next* time we're in Spokane we'll make that special trip into Coeur d' Alene," I kidded.

He gave me a familiar smile and said, "I'm a patient man."

We quickly found the park where the reunion was being held, and as we were setting our crock-pot full of calico beans on the buffet table, my mom walked over to Ed and gave him a big hug. Beaming, she said, "Welcome to the family, son!" and

13

sauntered off to join the others. Did she know something we didn't know?

Ed and I took seats beside my Uncle Jack to enjoy the wonderful bounty of food prepared by food lovin' Belles family cooks. Jack squinted as he gave Ed "the once over" as though he was examining the inner workings of a pocket watch. He chortled approvingly in Ed's direction, "Congratulations, son! Heard you two tied the knot in Coeur d' Alene this morning!"

Ah, that explained Mom's, "Welcome to the family!" comment.

A cool mist billowed up from Spokane Falls that same evening, as Ed and I were enjoying a leisurely time on the outside deck at Clinkendagger Restaurant. We were awestruck by the beautiful backdrop of a flame-colored sunset that reflected off the shiny rocks lining the steep riverbanks.

Ed was feeling especially full of himself with the warm welcomes of my family and all the good-natured kidding surrounding our "quickie" marriage in Coeur d' Alene.

Ed didn't know it, but that very afternoon I'd made the decision as to when we'd be getting married. And, I thought, "why not add to the fun that we'd endured at the family reunion?"

As Ed was savoring his first delectable bite of halibut, I tossed out the first piece of bait. "Did you like the calico bean dish that I made for the family reunion today?"

"Yeah, those beans were a hit with your family. They were really tasty. I'd like to have some right now to go with this halibut! You're a terrific cook, honey, I think everything you make is great!" He took another bite of fish.

I threw out the big one. "Since you like my cooking so much, what do you think of me making the same bean recipe for both our family's reunions next year and the year after and the year after?"

Ed's stunned look confirmed that he'd caught my meaning. He instantly stopped eating, and just stared at me smiling. A full minute went by before he resumed eating his fish - he still did not speak.

When he broke his silence he simply asked, "When?"

"What would you say about May of next year?" We both knew I was enjoying this.

He raised one eyebrow and playfully countered, "I'd like it to be sooner, how about March?"

Continuing on with my merriment, "November is my final offer! Weddings take a lot of planning, but I think I can pull it together by November...of this year!" I said laughing as I watched the thrilled expression on Ed's face.

We relished in the moment, knowing that together we'd just attended our first of many family reunions. The calico beans would be served at our future family gatherings always reminding us of that special evening overlooking Spokane Falls, when I said, "Yes!"

Family Reunion Calico Beans

½ pound bacon, diced, browned and drained
1½ cup yellow onion, diced
½ cup granulated sugar
1 tablespoon dry mustard
1 tablespoon vinegar
1 - 29 ounce can pork & beans, drained
2 - 15 ounce cans red kidney beans, drained
1 - 15 ounce can baby lima beans, black-eyed peas
    or garbanzo beans, drained
½ pound hamburger, crumbled, browned and drained
½ cup catsup
½ cup brown sugar, packed
1 teaspoon salt
½ teaspoon liquid smoke (optional)
12 ounces beer (optional)

Brown bacon and hamburger in a large skillet, drain in a colander, and rinse under hot water, if desired. Spray a 3-quart casserole dish with cooking spray; place all ingredients in baking dish, cover and bake for 1 hour at 350° or place all ingredients in crock-pot and cook on low for 8 hours. Makes 12 to 16 servings as a side dish or 8 to10 servings as a main dish served with hot corn bread.

This recipe comes from the kitchen of my mom, Betty Belles, Federal Way, Washington.

Ah...the Power of the Cheese Ball

When was the last time you served a cheese ball at a dinner party? 1978 perhaps? Some of you are probably rolling your eyes and saying, "Cheese ball? Ugh!"

The cheese ball was once a popular hors d'oeuvre, but in recent years, it has fallen into disfavor. I believe it's time to take a fresh look at cheese balls and logs because with the new low-fat and fat-free products, and a touch of imagination, they can be made at home with delicious, low-fat results. It's my goal to bring the cheese ball back to center stage on our appetizer tables.

Over the past 20 years we've all become more watchful of calories, fat and sodium. It's my belief that high fat content is the main reason we avoid serving cheese balls or cheese logs to our guests.

Often commercially made cheese balls are prepared with processed cheese and coated with stale walnuts, and they're laden with preservatives and sodium, which make them less than desirable.

With a little creativity, making your own cheese balls and logs at home can be a lot of fun. They're easy to assemble, a Godsend for the hostess, and they require only a few ingredients. However, the biggest plus is being able to control the sodium and fat levels.

Cheese balls and logs can be made with various combinations of cream cheese. There are 9.5 grams of fat, 6 grams of fat, and 0 grams of fat in 2 tablespoons (1 ounce) of regular cream cheese; Neufchatel cream cheese (or light cream cheese); and fat free cream cheese, respectively. Often, I choose a combination of light and fat-free cream cheese for my cheese balls to reduce the fat content. I did just that in making Sara Keifer's Special Cheese Ball with 1-8 ounce package of Neufchatel cream cheese and 1-8 ounce package fat free Philadelphia Cream Cheese. By making this substitution, I've saved approximately 2.3 grams of fat per serving.

Garnishing the cheese ball is the most creative part! Instead of rolling the cheese ball in walnuts, try chopped pine nuts, perhaps pumpkin or sunflower seeds; chopped fresh parsley or cilantro; minced celery, or simply leave the outside of the cheese ball plain. If you want a more elegant presentation, make 1" miniature cheese balls, roll in desired garnish and insert a toothpick into each tiny ball, serve with crackers or veggies for bite-sized servings.

You're probably asking, "What about crackers?" Why use them? Melba Rounds and Rye Crisps are two of my favorite low-fat choices. Other healthy, low-calorie compliments for the cheese ball are vegetables, which might include cherry tomatoes, zucchini, jicima and cucumber discs; green, red and yellow bell pepper strips, celery and carrot sticks, or small crisp butter or endive lettuce leaves.

I'm sharing three cheese ball recipes with you that always bring me compliments. My mother can take a bow for Betty B's Salmon Cheese Ball – I'll say it's tasty but I'd never call it fishy! I've been making my Hidden Valley Ranch Cheese Ball for so long that I can't begin to remember its origin. However, when my guests have all departed there is never a speck of it left in the dish - especially if my daughter, Holly, is in attendance. Sara Keifer's Special Cheese Ball comes from my 15-year-old step niece. Her recipe is a showstopper and it could be the center stage appetizer at your next party.

Betty B's Salmon Cheese Ball

8 ounces cream cheese, softened
6 ounces smoked salmon, flaked
1½ teaspoons lemon juice
½ teaspoon dried minced onions
½ cup walnuts or pecans, coarsely chopped
Fresh parsley and lemon slices (optional)

Mix cream cheese, salmon, lemon juice and onions together until well blended. Form into a ball and roll in nuts. Wrap securely in plastic wrap. Garnish with parsley and lemon slices (optional). Chill 4 hours. Remove from refrigerator 30 minutes before serving. Makes 1 cheese ball and serves 14 generously (2 crackers, each with ½ ounce cheese spread = one serving). Serve with variety of snack crackers or raw vegetables.

Hidden Valley Ranch Cheese Ball

1 – 1 ounce package Hidden Valley Ranch Dressing, dry
¼ cup butter, softened
8 ounces cream cheese, softened
½ cup walnuts or pecans, coarsely chopped
Fresh parsley, cilantro or candied cherries (optional)

Mix dry Hidden Valley Ranch Dressing, butter and cream cheese together until well blended. Form into a ball and roll in nuts. Wrap securely in plastic wrap. Garnish with parsley, cilantro or candied cherries. Chill 4 to 6 hours. Remove from refrigerator 30 minutes before serving. Makes 1 cheese ball and serves 10 (2 crackers, each with ½ ounce cheese spread = one serving). Serve with variety of snack crackers.

Sara Keifer's Special Cheese Ball

16 ounces cream cheese, softened
2 - 2.5 ounce packages chipped beef (i.e., Buddig), chopped fine
1 bunch green onions with tops, chopped fine
1 tablespoon mayonnaise
¼ teaspoon garlic powder
¾ cup pecans, coarsely chopped
Fresh parsley or cilantro (optional)

Mix cream cheese, lunchmeat, green onions, mayonnaise and garlic powder together until well blended. Form into one large ball (or two small balls) and roll in chopped pecans. Garnish with fresh parsley or cilantro. Wrap in plastic wrap. Chill for 4 hours. Remove from refrigerator 30 minutes before serving. Makes 1 large cheese ball and serves 24 generously (2 crackers, each with ½ ounce cheese spread = one serving). Serve with variety of snack crackers, celery sticks or zucchini discs.

Chapter Two

Serving-up Soups & Salads

On occasion, when my spirit needs nourishment, I get out my crock pot and begin chopping the ingredients to prepare a hearty chili or a flavorful soup. I use what I call the antique spices - dried rosemary, sage, bay leaf...the herbs and spices my grandmother dried in the sun on a mesh rack and stored on her pantry shelf to be used for seasoning foods throughout the year.

Similarly, when I begin filling my wooden salad bowl with crispy vegetables and leafy greens, my mind wanders back to a time when women gathered fresh lettuce from their vegetable gardens, when they hand-picked tomatoes from the plants that grew just outside their kitchen doors, or when they prepared a fruit salad with weighty melons lugged-in from a hot dusty field.

Whether I'm dicing green chiles to put in Southwest Meets Northwest White Chili, trimming spinach for Pendleton Spinach Salad, or slicing sweet juicy watermelon for Father's Day Fruit Salad preparing soups and salads makes me feel like I've shared the afternoon with my grandmother.

Cynthia Briggs

Biting into a snappy salad or smelling "antique" spices simmering in homemade soup connects me with my roots, and the kitchen queens from whom I've fashioned my culinary expertise.

CB

Southwest Meets Northwest

The Carlsbad Public Library was my first stop after being asked to write a cooking column for the Current Argus Newspaper. Donna, the librarian at the Information Desk, raised her eyebrows and asked curiously, "How long did you live in Seattle? What brought you to New Mexico?"

As Donna listened earnestly I explained. "The Pacific Northwest was my home for 42 years. My husband, Ed, who is an engineer, made a job change and the next thing I knew we were camping in our new house in Carlsbad waiting, not so patiently, for a moving van to pull up in our driveway. Moving to the Southwest is a big change for us and it's an adventure that we're embracing whole-heartedly. We've met friendly people, who have enthusiastically welcomed us into the community."

"It's surprising to find restaurants that are closed on the weekend - I don't think anything ever closes in Seattle! And my husband's grueling 60-minute commute to work has been replaced with a leisurely 15-minute drive. We're enjoying the slower pace here, along with the reduced stress level that accompanies it."

"For the past year I've been writing a cooking column called "Kitchen Corner" for a Federal Way, Washington, newspaper. When it was definite that we'd be relocating to Carlsbad, I sent an introduction letter, along with some clips of my work, to the publisher of the Current Argus, with the hope of continuing to do the two things I love to do most – write and cook."

"So, the reason I'm here today is to gather research material for my new assignment. Do you have any cookbooks that will help me understand the essence of Southwest cuisine?" I asked. "I'm in panic mode because I've got some fast learning to do in order to meet my first deadline."

Donna smiled and patiently said, "We have several outstanding, Southwestern cookbooks that you'll enjoy, and I'd suggest you check with the cooperative extension service, it's just a few blocks from here. The extension service can help you with local crop information and harvesting data. They might even have some recipes to get you started."

Cathy, at the extension service was as helpful as the librarian had been. I left the building with my arms wrapped around two weeks of reading material. Southwestern cooking presented a steep learning curve mostly because of the frequent use of peppers of various sorts in many entrees, breads and salads, but I was determined to "shave the mountain cliffs down to hilly slopes."

By the following day I'd perused most of the books, pamphlets and folders I'd collected. While looking through the recipes in the Southwest cookbooks, I asked myself, "What's so different about the food we prepare in Washington and what we eat in New Mexico?"

I recalled that friends describe my cooking style as "home cooking" and "comfort food." I took some time to flip through the standby recipes in my recipe box and I asked myself, "What were some favorites that I put in my Seattle column?" Almond Shrimp Salad, Crab Shell Soup, Easy Oven Baked Barbecued Ribs, Sweet and Sour Chicken, Blackberry Pie and Old Fashioned Oatmeal Cake came to mind. I realized that anyone who likes food would be delighted to run a taste test on these basic favorites – regardless of where they live.

After being all a twitter, I decided this was an exhilarating opportunity for me to write and cook in a new locale where I could explore the regional foods and experiment with unique seasonings. And, it would be fun adding a new twist to some old favorite recipes.

I think you'll enjoy the following White Chili recipe, which I frequently prepared on rainy days in the Pacific Northwest. However, I've christened it with a new name hoping for a successful blast-off of my column in the sunny Southwest.

Southwest Meets Northwest White Chili

8 ounces pinto beans, dry
3 chicken bouillon cubes
1 clove fresh garlic, minced
3 to 4 cups water
1 pound chicken breast, cubed
½ to 1 cup green chiles, roasted, peeled and diced
1 teaspoon ground cumin
1½ teaspoons dry oregano leaves, crushed
⅛ teaspoon cloves
¼ teaspoon cayenne pepper
1 cup dry onion, finely chopped
Tabasco and parsley, optional

Place pinto beans in a large, heavy simmering pot, cover beans with water and soak overnight. Drain water from the beans; add garlic, bouillon cubes and 3 to 4 cups water; simmer on medium-low heat. When beans are almost tender; fry the cubed chicken breast in hot oil until pink goes away; drain off excess oil and add chicken to beans; add the green chiles, cumin, oregano, cloves, cayenne pepper and dry onion. Simmer for approximately 30 minutes or until onions and beans are tender. Serve piping hot, garnished with a splash of Tabasco and fresh parsley or cilantro. Makes 4 generous servings.

Optional: Just before serving, put ⅓ of the white chili into the blender. Blend until smooth; return to chili pot and stir. I use this simple technique for most soup to give it more body without using thickeners. Also, this chili cooks up nicely in the crock pot.

Shrimp is a Great Idea - in Washington State

Yesterday when I purchased shrimp to make my husband's favorite Almond Shrimp Salad, I recalled October 1998 when my husband-to-be and I traveled to Bovey, Minnesota, so my future mother-in-law and I could meet for the first time. I knew this initial introduction could affect our married life, for better or worse, for many years to come. During this trip, to add to my already self-imposed jitters, I planned on showing off my culinary talents by preparing dinner to celebrate Mom's 86th birthday.

Was I any different than any other woman? I kept telling myself that most women want their mothers-in-law to know that their sons are in good hands. It's important that "Mother" knows we daughters-in-law *always* keep our houses glistening clean. We stress to her that with nary a whimper we *always* drive past the malls – keeping the Platinum Visa Cards in our wallets. We *always* remember lightly starched shirts for her corporate dynamo. And we *always* prepare healthy, lip-smacking meals that will keep her handsome son slender and virile, just like the meals Mother *always* served.

My plan was to make Almond Shrimp Salad for the birthday bash. "I'll dazzle her for sure!" I thought. Mom would know that her Sonny Boy wouldn't be eating Hungry-man Frozen Dinners.

When "Eddie" and I arrived at Mom's home, nestled on the quiet shore of Riley Lake, I quickly ascertained that Ed's Mom was every bit as precious as he had related to me. She squeezed my hand firmly and said, "Welcome to the family dear. You can call me Mom." My spirits soared.

However, the next day my confidence began to falter when we asked the butcher at "Our Last Hope Grocery" where we could find shrimp meat. "Vat ez zat?" the butcher enunciated slowly with what I surmised to be a Minnesota accent.

"You know, the baby shrimp." Ed was suddenly using pigeon sign language.

"We're from Seattle and we buy shrimp in the fresh fish section of our food market." I feared we were losing the butcher.

"You must sell shrimp out of a different department – like the deli section or perhaps there's a fish market in town...somewhere...anywhere?" Ed and I trailed off in unison.

"Look over zar in zee freezer section." The butcher pointed. We found the frozen shrimp but it was imported from...where?

What sure-fire dinner could I recall from my recipes, which were in Washington tucked away in my wooden box marked "EATS?"

Mom looked at me with curiosity when, on her birthday afternoon, I stuffed two lemons into the cavity of a large baking hen and slid it into a 450 degree oven. I silently thanked Martha Stewart for *always* being on television and I said to Mom, "Baked chicken *always* hits the spot."

Almond Shrimp Salad

> 1 head iceberg lettuce
> 5 to 6 green onions
> 1 - 3 ounce package Ramen, crush noodles into
>   small pieces, discard seasoning packet
> 4 tablespoons butter
> 2 tablespoons sesame seeds
> ½ cup blanched almonds, slivered
> 1 pound tiny salad shrimp, drained

Cut washed lettuce into bite-size pieces and place sliced onions in a large salad bowl. Melt butter in sauté pan over medium-low heat. Add crushed noodles to butter and sauté until lightly brown.

Add almonds and sesame seeds to noodles, and continue browning. Remove from burner when noodles mixture is well toasted and set aside. Spread drained shrimp on top of lettuce and onions. Sprinkle noodle mixture over the shrimp. Toss lightly. Serve with dressing below or use seasoned rice vinegar.

Dressing

½ teaspoon sea salt
Freshly ground pepper to taste
¼ teaspoon Tabasco pepper sauce
2 tablespoons sugar
2 tablespoons tarragon vinegar
¼ cup vegetable oil
Combine ingredients in a shaker container and mix well.

Wild Italian Stallion Salad Hit of the Party

Ed lit the white taper candles, which accented a Victorian birdcage centerpiece on the dining room table in a soft romantic glow. Several couples were coming over to celebrate Valentine's Day with pink champagne, coffee and my own personal rendition of tiramisu.

"You've set a beautiful table tonight, Honey. Your attention to detail and setting the mood must be why your parties are always so successful," Ed commented as he filled the heart-shaped crystal candy dishes with Hershey's Kisses.

"I think every party needs at least one thread of originality to make it memorable for the guests. One unusual element should be created by the hostess and there's always a 'wrinkle' that's governed by fate!" I replied. "I've held some great parties but I've also had my share of close calls! Each party, wild or mild, has taught me something valuable about entertaining."

"I'm surprised to hear you say that. Can you give me an example of a 'close call'?" Ed asked, looking perplexed.

"Do you remember the progressive dinners that were so popular back in the 70s?" I asked him.

"I'm not sure. What's a progressive dinner?" Ed asked.

"It's a dinner where the guests travel to a different house for each course." I replied, noticing that Ed had started enjoying the Hershey's Kisses.

I continued, "One of my early experiences with party planning involved a progressive dinner. A small group of us were responsible for planning the first dinner. We had five different houses; each host house would serve one course. We neglected to determine ahead of time which courses would be accompanied with wine. Consequently, wine was served with every course, including dessert. By the end of the evening, we

29

'giddily' deemed the party a success, not even considering the food!"

"Worse things could have happened!" Ed replied. Another Hershey's Kiss disappeared.

My Old English feasts were probably the most unusual, but interesting doesn't always guarantee success. One of the biggest lessons I learned about party planning occurred with my first medieval dinner.

Medieval feasts had a built-in "wrinkle" because no silverware was placed on the table. Fingers and hands had to be used as eating utensils.

I'd set a medieval scene beginning with the dining room table situated in front of the fireplace. A blazing, crackling fire in the fireplace helped spirit the imagination toward castles inhabited with lords and ladies. The linens were in shades of ruby red and a country basket overflowed with napkins denoting the centerpiece. Pewter wine goblets helped set the period and large, hammered-copper bowls were placed about the table for discarding bones and artichoke leaves.

To kick the meal off on a lively note, I'd wait for my guests to notice there weren't any eating implements on the table. "Oh, I don't have any silverware!" the first guest would say. "Gosh! None of us have any silverware. May I help? I can get some from the kitchen," another guest would offer.

At this point I'd break the unsuspecting news. "Tonight we're going to revel in a medieval feast. Our fingers and hands served as eating utensils in medieval times…that's what we shall experience this evening. So, roll up your sleeves and prepare yourself for a finger food feast!" Some guests would gasp at the mere thought and others would giggle.

I relished in presenting the "no silverware" twist to my guests. However, I unintentionally set myself up for an unexpected foible when I decided to serve my Wild Italian Stallion Salad. Fortunately, my guests were good sports and accustomed to my unpredictable parties, and with the shocking manners of medieval barbarians they threw themselves into solving the besieging challenge of dining without silverware.

The menu for medieval dinners usually consisted of finger friendly foods: corn on the cob, barbecued pork ribs and chicken wings, roasted turkey legs, steamed French artichokes, golden loaves of un-sliced sheepherder's bread, crispy carrots and celery sticks; the addition of my Wild Italian Stallion Salad became the evening's bugaboo.

Midway through dinner a guest shouted, "Hey, try eating the salad like this!" Using his hands and a carrot stick he scooped salad onto the pepperoni slices that were in the salad, making kind of a mini-pepperoni taco. The other guests quickly adapted his technique! That night I was surprised to learn how making a party blunder such as using an unfriendly finger food could turn out to be the highlight of the evening given the guests' sense of adventure.

Although I believe quirks and wrinkles can make a party memorable, I removed salad from my standard Old English feast menu. My Wild Italian Stallion Salad remains one of my favorite main dish salads to serve to a hungry crowd, and a recipe I'd like to pass on to you. It's packed with spicy pepperoni, Mozzarella cheese, marinated artichoke hearts and olives, tossed together to satisfy the most vigorous appetite. I suggest that you serve it with crusty garlic bread and chilled salad forks. The latter will help compensate for any "wrinkles" that invite themselves to dinner.

Wild Italian Stallion Salad

2 cups macaroni twists, drained and rinsed
½ cup Italian dressing, divided
1 - 6 ounce jar marinated artichoke hearts, drained (reserve liquid), cut into bite sized pieces
1 large bunch red leaf lettuce, washed and broken into bit-size pieces
1 cup Mozzarella cheese, grated
1 - 6 ounce package thin sliced Italian pepperoni
1½ cups fresh sliced mushrooms
10 cherry tomatoes, halved

½ cup coarsely grated Parmesan cheese
1 - 4 ounce can sliced olives, drained

Place prepared macaroni twists in a zip-lock bag; stir in ¼ cup Italian dressing. Refrigerate for 1 hour or longer.

Drain artichokes; reserve marinade and set aside. In a large salad bowl add artichokes, macaroni twists, artichoke hearts, lettuce, Mozzarella cheese, pepperoni, mushrooms, tomatoes, Parmesan cheese, and olives. Toss well; drizzle with reserved artichoke marinade and remaining ¼ cup Italian dressing; toss thoroughly. Serve immediately with garlic bread. Makes 4 servings.

Good Clam Chowder is as fun as a Trip to Beach

"**I thought a Geoduck was the Washington** State bird!" quipped my husband as we meandered along State Route 12, near Montesano, Washington, on our way to Ocean Shores.

I doubled over with laughter nearly hitting my head on the dashboard. Humor that catches me by surprise always strikes me the funniest.

"Why would a city boy like me, from Chicago, think a geoduck was anything other than a duck?" He asked, trying to portray a naïve landlubber.

He had me caught up in his comedic routine. Then he threw in the clincher that put me over the edge. "So, how do you cook the feathers?"

After regaining my composure I began to actually think about the word g-e-o-d-u-c-k. I'd never really *heard* the duck in geoduck. Geoduck was just a funny name for a colossal clam. I'd never associated the geoduck with any kind of fowl – even though my own 10 toes had begun growing webs from living in our "good-weather-for-ducks" climate.

To get some background information on the geoduck, I talked with Kelly Curtis, a geoduck expert. As serious as Kelly is about her geoduck studies, she demonstrated that she's maintained her sense of humor about the geoduck by writing a humorous little ditty that's worth noting:

"Well, he hasn't got a front and he hasn't got a back.
He doesn't know Donald, and he doesn't go 'quack'."

Digging-up geoducks can be a thankless effort because they hide so deep below the surface of the sand. My family has always gone digging for clams. If you've never been and the opportunity strikes – go for it! It's great family fun!

With our clam shovels in hand, I recall descending upon the cold, foggy shore of Pacific Beach, Washington. We'd gently tap our toe on each wet dimpled imprinted in the sand so we'd know where to begin digging. Shivering wet and with salty grit packed between our toes we'd trudge back to the camper with our daily limit. Our reward was a rich, succulent pot of steaming clam chowder.

Yes, we waged war on the elusive clam and many of us returned to camp with our fingers sliced open from the clam's only weapon - its shell. It was not uncommon to misjudge the whereabouts of the shifty critter as it dug furiously in its downward plight for survival. Their diggers were fast and many of them escaped our shovels; but the ones we took prisoner were a shellfish delight that were delicious to the last drop of nectar!

I've been clam digging perhaps a hundred times in my life and I've never encountered anyone digging-up a geoduck generally they're safe covered beneath deep water and sand.

Kelly tells me she goes diving in the frigid waters of Puget Sound for the geoduck, saving herself the trouble of having to "dig clear to China!"

Thanks, Kelly, but I think I'll stick to hunting for razor clams on a breezy beach with my head above water.

For my clam chowder, I've always used ground razor clams, canned minced clams, or ground geoduck - all are equally tasty.

After discussing with my husband, the feasibility of the geoduck being related to the poultry family, I think perhaps I should give Kelly a call and ask her if she's ever unearthed a geoduck cloaked in feathers instead of a shell. Perhaps, I shouldn't have been making assumptions all these years!

Pacific Beach Clam Chowder

½ pound bacon, fried crisp, drained and chopped (set
   aside)
4 medium potatoes, cubed
1 cup dry onion, chopped
½ cup celery, chopped
½ cup carrots, grated
1 teaspoon sea salt
¼ teaspoon fresh ground pepper
1 tablespoon parsley
3 - 6 ½ ounce cans chopped clams
OR 1 ½ cups fresh razor, manila or geoduck clams
1 -15 ounce can creamed corn
12 ounces evaporated milk

Add potatoes, onion, celery, carrots, salt and pepper to a heavy Dutch oven; add enough water (about 1 cup) to *not quite* cover the vegetables. Cover pan with lid, bring to a boil and simmer for about 15 minutes (or until potatoes are cooked but still firm).

Blend 2 cups of the cooked potato mixture through a blender until smooth; return blended mixture to Dutch oven. Add parsley, crisped bacon, corn, and canned clams (with juice). Heat thoroughly - do not boil. Remove from the heat; add evaporated milk, stir to blend.

Garnish with additional parsley, if desired. Serve with oyster crackers or fresh sourdough bread. Makes 8-10 servings

Any Way You Slice It, Tomatoes are a Delicious Fruit

"Bob, slow down! Now get ready to pull over! There's a stand around the next corner. We can't miss it!" Mom chirped at Dad in the front seat of our 1961 Pontiac, Bonneville.

"Oh hell! Don't you already have enough tomatoes to keep you canning for a week?" He grumbled back at her maintaining the tradition of their canning season conversation.

My brother, Randy, and I whined from a dusty back seat, while we zigzagged over curvy country roads in a dauntless search of hefty Beefsteak and delicate Early Girl tomatoes. Mom wasn't particular. Common tomatoes that could be preserved in a Mason jar, eaten out of hand, or frozen in Tupperware, were packed in the trunk. Each white sign that read FRUIT in bold red letters, brought hope of finding the juiciest, freshest, plumpest, and the best-priced "maters." We froze em', canned em' in jars, dried em' on racks and pickled em'.

My mother and grandmother worked wonders with the red, bodacious fruit. I grew up knowing that tomatoes are mouth-watering whether they're steamed, sautéed, stewed or stuffed. They're delectable made into tomato sauce, puree, or paste, which we combined with an array of Italian spices and simmered into red sauces to pour over pizza and pasta dishes. Nowadays it's become trendy to eat them sun-dried or kabob-style from the grill.

I recall one year when Mom and Gramma made a concoction they called tomato preserves. "Nothing like em'!" Gramma said, as she served herself a sample, spreading it on a saltine cracker, smacking her lips and winking from its apparent tartness.

It was ingrained in me to never waste a tomato and that included green tomatoes! Most of us have seen the movie

Fried Green Tomatoes, but have you heard of green tomato pie, pineapple-green tomato relish or green dilled tomatoes? Don't forget the all-American favorite - tomato catsup...available commercially in red, green, and purple!

Every year my spirits soar with the hope of an early harvest, and fond tomato memories of my family preserving fruits and vegetables begin dancing their way through my mind every spring when young green tomato plants begin making their appearances in the feed stores, nurseries and garden shops.

At the mere sight of tender tomato leaves, I begin recalling the good old days when tomato prices were scrawled on brown paper sacks hanging above rough-hewn wooden display bins. My family always made a beeline for the vegetable bin at any market that was filled to the top with juicy red giants – the really good kind of tomatoes that needed clumps of mud washed from their glossy skins. Sometimes in our haste we'd rush past the fresh tomatoes only to find them under heavily dampened gunnysacks, safe and secure from over-exposure to the sun and heat.

Remember that tomatoes are in season until the end of September. If you're lucky, you might discover a bushel or two at a roadside vegetable stand so "slow down and get ready to pull over. You don't want to miss them!"

Cynthia's Mm Mm Good Marinated Tomatoes

6 large tomatoes, sliced ½ inch thick

Marinade:
1 cup olive oil
¼ cup wine vinegar
1 teaspoon sea salt
1-2 tablespoons fresh basil, chopped
½ teaspoon dry mustard
¼ - ½ teaspoon black pepper, fresh ground
2 cloves garlic, minced
2 sprigs thyme, chopped

1 sprig marjoram, chopped
2 tablespoons scallions or green onions, using some
    green stem, chopped

Place sliced tomatoes in a large bowl. Combine marinade ingredients in a shaker, pour over sliced tomatoes, and gently stir. Cover tightly and marinate at least 1 hour before serving. Makes 8 generous servings.

Suggestions:

1) Fresh-from-the-vine tomatoes are a MUST for success with this recipe.
2) Cut calories in recipe by reducing olive oil to ½ cup and increasing wine vinegar to ½ cup.
3) Fresh herbs offer the best flavor for marinated tomatoes. However, dried herbs can be substituted when necessary. For 1 tablespoon of dried herb used, add 1 tablespoon water.
4) When the marinated tomatoes disappear, use the remaining marinade over salad greens. Mm good!
5) Serve marinated tomatoes with dollops of cottage cheese and croutons for a great dinner salad or light lunch.

Spinach Instincts

"Oh, I'm so sorry ma'am! Are you all right?" I apologized to the lady who I'd just sideswiped with my shopping cart in the produce department. "And, what about these AAA jumbo eggs? May I buy you another dozen?" I lamented, hoping to make amends.

"No, I'm fine and so are my eggs. Why did you nearly run me over just to get to the spinach?" The woman was understandably annoyed, but I surmised that she wasn't going to report me to anyone that would revoke my shopping privileges.

I'm the first to admit that my protecting and gathering instinct toward lush, bundles of tender spinach is too strong. There are two separate incidents, from past experiences, which nourish my unusual compulsion.

In 1971 my mother and I took a spur-of-the-moment trip to Pendleton, Oregon, to explore my birthplace. As it turned out, we got more than we'd bargained for when the radiator in my Matador station wagon boiled over because of a staggering heat wave that blanketed most of Eastern Oregon.

Four days into our visit the new radiator still hadn't arrived. The oppressive humidity made Mom's mood soar beyond testy and exploring had run its course. One afternoon we wandered into one of the small downtown diners to have lunch.

"Why, this spinach salad is delicious! Look at this...cashews, almonds, bacon, Jack cheese...and a hot poppy seed dressing," Mom remarked as she munched on the salad. "I'm going to get the recipe!" The heat was getting to her and she was cross about the delayed radiator repair...she was not a woman to be tarried with any longer.

Needless to say, we didn't make any friends in the diner that day. But, after subjecting the chef and the waiter to grueling interrogations, Mom came away with the spinach salad recipe. Oddly enough, the recipe served a whopping 50 people.

Undaunted, Mom immediately put pencil to paper and whittled the recipe down to family size servings.

Thereafter, every spring, Mom and I waited for my family's vegetable garden to produce spinach for our fabulous Pendleton Spinach Salad.

My children were surprisingly enthusiastic about the experience of growing fresh vegetables. Mostly, the kids delighted in chasing the birds away from the corn seeds and checking to see when the pumpkin seeds popped their heads out from under the rich dark soil. Invariably, we'd hear, "WOW, this carrot is the granddaddy of them all!"

"It's time to fertilize the garden, kids. And I think you're both old enough to do the job without supervision. Just remember: 1 teaspoon of fertilizer granules sprinkled on the dirt beside each plant. Okay?" Their little heads nodded up and down in agreement. "Ah, how they loved to help the garden grow," I thought, beaming inside with maternal pride.

"Mom, we're done! Can we go over and play with Seth?" My future agriculturists asked wistfully from the back porch.

"That was fast! Sure, go ahead. Unless, of course, Seth's mom chases you home earlier," I added.

Shortly after the children left, I went outside to hoe weeds. "Oh, my gosh! What have they done?" I shrieked from the garden gate. "Oh, I thought they knew better than to do this!" I was near tears.

The kids had used a full 25-pound sack of vegetable fertilizer in one application. The empty bag lay deflated next to the cucumber plants. Suspiciously, the spinach had taken the brunt of the attack. I found sand pails and shovels carelessly left at the end of the spinach row. The spinach seed package, in spite of witnessing the ugly crime, remained on its stick sprightly identifying the destined-to-die spinach.

"It can't be true. All this time and care to raise succulent spinach down the tube." I muttered to myself in disbelief.

Needless to say, it was a sparse year for fresh, garden spinach, which left Mom and me with a deep-seated fear of finding spinach on an endangered vegetable list. But, my recent incident in the produce aisle has me thinking that my passion to obtain the leafy, green veggie has gone a bit too far!

Pendleton Spinach Salad

1 bunch fresh spinach, washed, cleaned and broken
    into bite-size pieces
¼ pound bacon, cooked and crumbled
2 boiled eggs, peeled and sliced
¼ cup roasted almonds, chopped coarsely
¼ cup roasted cashews, chopped coarsely
¼ pound Jack cheese, shredded
1 cup fresh mushrooms, sliced

Toss ingredients together in a large salad bowl and serve immediately with Hot Poppy Seed Dressing. Makes 6 servings.

Hot Poppy Seed Dressing

Combine in a saucepan: ½ cup sugar, ¼ cup red wine vinegar, ½ cup salad oil, 1 teaspoon dry mustard, 1 teaspoon poppy seeds, 1 teaspoon minced onion, ½ teaspoon salt. Heat mixture over medium heat (do not boil) and serve over salad.

Crabmeat is a Costly Treat

Kathy, a previous co-worker of mine, tells about the year when the price of Dungeness crab was at a market low of $1 per *crab*, and one could easily take one's pick of the largest crab scooting around in the bottom of the tub. In fact, the price was so rock-bottom that crabbers found it necessary and lucrative to sell their live catches on the street from the back of their trucks.

"I'd never bought a live crab before," Kathy said. "The crabber instructed me on how to cook them, and I felt especially adventurous that day; I bought 4 of the bug-eyed, pre-historic looking creatures to take home for dinner. It sounded easy enough, just drop the chosen crab into a pot of rapidly boiling water and simmer it until its shell turns red."

"Have you ever had to chase a crab around your kitchen? Or worse yet, have you ever been chased around your own kitchen by a crab?" Kathy asked me with a mischievous lilt in her voice.

"Well, I discovered the hard way," she explained, "that a crab needs to be dropped into the boiling water on its back. For when I dropped the first crab into the pot facedown, it quickly climbed back up the inside of the pot, hoisted itself over the top-edge of the pan and landed, 'ker-plop,' onto the floor. Its pincers were going, 'clack, clack,' as the aggravated crab chased me screaming across the kitchen to the safety of a nearby bedroom." Kathy howled with laughter as she recalled the incident.

"When I finally got the nerve to leave the bedroom, I chased him around the kitchen, grabbed the partially scalded cantankerous crab from behind and quickly dropped him into the pot...on his back. Victory was mine!" She gallantly announced.

"Without doubt, it was well worth the skirmish to have fresh cracked crabmeat for dinner that night, and at such a

42

ridiculously low price!" she added. "However, I think that kind of market low price is gone forever."

I agree with Kathy, inexpensive crabmeat prices are non-existent these days. No matter how you weigh the critter - crab is going cost you. But for seafood fans, the following Crabmeat Pasta-Shell Soup is oh so worth it, even at today's exorbitant prices.

A dear friend, and fellow crabmeat lover, who makes crab soup at her annual Christmas dinner every year, shared this recipe with me about 25 years ago. In exchange for her recipe, I loaned her my china to use at her large dinner parties as we both had the same unusual pattern.

After preparing her crab soup recipe for all these years, I decided the succulent soup deserved the honor of having its own special bowls. Slurping it down from ordinary bowls didn't feel right to me. So, I splurged and bought sparkling new, French white, wide rimmed, soup bowls with a delicate delphinium blue trim. Crabmeat Pasta-Shell Soup, in our house, is now an occasion.

So don't go out and pawn any of your valuables in order to buy the crab for this soup. With some creative economizing or just plain splurging, you'll find a way to fit it into your budget. And, don't new soup bowls sound appealing?

Crabmeat Pasta-Shell Soup

¼ cup onion, chopped
¼ cup green pepper, chopped (optional)
¼ cup celery, diced
1 to 2 tablespoons margarine or butter
3½ cups chicken broth
1 cup ripe tomato, peeled and crushed
¼ cup conchigliette (tiny shells) pasta
1 tablespoon parsley, snipped
½ teaspoon salt
Freshly ground pepper to taste

6 to 8 ounces fresh crabmeat, cartilage and shell removed **OR** 2 - 6 ounce cans crabmeat, drained and rinsed

In a large saucepan, sauté onion, green pepper and celery in margarine until tender but not brown. Add broth, tomatoes, conchigliette, parsley, salt and pepper; bring to boiling. Cover and simmer for 30 minutes. Add crab and simmer 5 minutes longer. Serve immediately. Makes 6 to 8 servings.

Recipe comes from the kitchen of Cheryl Burke, Kent, Washington.

Crabmeat Pasta-Shell Soup is so rich and filling it can easily be served as a main entrée. Accompanied with a small dinner salad, fresh sourdough bread and your favorite white wine, you'll have a completely wonderful dinner.

Dad's Case of 'Fishing Fever' Inspires Love of Salmon Dishes

Fishing fever bit my dad, R. D. Belles, during his late 20s. We'd notice that he was experiencing a flare-up of what we called "salmon fever" when his sleeping and eating patterns took a sudden turn. Normally, Dad moaned at the buzz of an alarm clock and slept in until noon whenever he got the chance, and routinely he began every day with the hardiest of breakfasts.

But when he pointed the truck and boat trailer toward his favorite fishing haunts out on the tip of the Olympic Peninsula in Washington State, R.D.'s usual sleeping and eating patterns became drastically altered.

He'd spring out of bed at 3:30 a.m. "No time for breakfast. I have to get out there and wake up those Kings!" he'd whisper to us slipping out of the cabin like a cat sneaking into the night.

Well after dark we'd see the running lights of his boat, *Bob-Bet* bumping against the dock. R.D.'s broad smile glinting through the darkness told us his catch for the day was abundant! Unconcerned about whiskers sprouting from his unshaved chin, he'd flop into a chair at the kitchen table and say, "I'm as hungry as a bear coming out of hibernation!" Over a platter of pan-fried red potatoes and shaker fish he'd strategize the next day's outing.

Dad took fishing far more serious than anyone else in the family. Once, while fishing with him, I became severely seasick and begged to go back to shore. Foreboding walls of water rocked the 26' craft back and forth among the powerful waves. *Bob-Bet* lifted WAY UP and then plummeted WAY DOWN, between the rollers. R.D. patiently puffed on his pipe and said, "Oh, you'll be okay, you've just had too much motion today." Sundown was the only good excuse for Dad to return to shore.

Once, I asked Dad if he'd bring back a dogfish (which is a small shark) for me to fry up for dinner. I'd heard that dogfish had a unique texture partnered with a surprisingly non-fishy flavor. He hit the ceiling. "I won't have the damn stinkn' things in my boat. You can't kill em'- even with a club! If you can't kill em', then ya can't eat em'!" he blasted at me.

Knowing this was a hurdle that would be impossible to jump, I persuaded my Uncle Ken, who was also curious about the feasibility of dogfish and chips for dinner, to bring me a large, fresh-from-the-sea dogfish the next time he went fishing with Dad.

Dad was furious with his older brother and acted like Ken was a traitor to the Salmon Fishing Hall of Fame. The next day I barbecued a small Coho salmon for Dad and deep-fried the dogfish for my more adventurous guests. Dad showed up for dinner that infamous afternoon, but it was the first vegetarian meal I ever saw him eat, and he never ate fish at my house again! Oh yes, the dogfish was delicious!

Bobbi's Salmon & Green Bean Salad

    8 to 10 ounces canned, baked or poached salmon, chilled, de-boned and flaked
    3 to 4 cups fresh green beans, snapped into 2" pieces, steamed to almost done, cooled
    1 small Vidalia or Walla Walla sweet onion, separated into rings
    1½ cups iceberg lettuce, shredded (optional)
    1 medium tomato (sliced) or cherry tomatoes (optional)

Dressing

    2 tablespoons white wine vinegar
    1 tablespoon olive oil
    2 teaspoons lemon juice, fresh squeezed
    2 teaspoons water

4 tablespoons fresh basil, chopped
½ - 1 teaspoon sea salt
Cracked pepper to taste
1 or 2 cloves garlic, minced

Toss salmon, beans and onion together in a large bowl. Measure vinegar, oil, lemon juice, water, basil, salt, pepper, and garlic into shaker container. Shake well. Pour dressing over salmon mixture and toss. Cover and refrigerate for 2 hours before serving.

Serve on bed of shredded lettuce. Garnish with tomatoes. Serves 3 to 4 as main dish salad or 8 to 9 as side salads.

Suggestions:
- If you're in a pinch, you can successfully substitute: 2 tablespoons dried basil that has been soaked in 2 tablespoons warm water for the fresh basil.
- This salad can be made-up the day before you intend to serve it. In fact, it enhances the flavor; just be sure to withhold the iceberg lettuce until serving.
- Only use fresh cooked green beans - canned green beans are too overcooked.
- Served with your favorite white wine and French bread, this makes an unusual main dish meal that's easy on the waistline.

This recipe comes from the kitchen of Bobbi Powell, Federal Way, Washington.

Cynthia Briggs

The King of Melons

"You're such a wiggle-worm!" Gramma said. Then she'd hug me and rest her hands lovingly on my tiny shoulders as a gentle reminder for me to stay near the house. My desire was to bolt past the red raspberry canes with their plump juicy berries, and zigzag between the towering pea patch poles to meet Grandpa at the watermelon field gate.

"Here comes Grandpa! Look Gramma! The melon he picked today is a whopper!" I touched my fingertips to my mouth and sucked in quickly attempting to keep from drooling. The foretaste of the succulent melon-of-the-day was too great and I wiped the dribble from my chin with my dusty palm.

"Just be patient young'n. He's on his way!" Gramma said. My back pressed against her well-worn cotton apron while both of us waited in the blistering August sun.

I squirmed with anticipation as Grandpa lumbered toward the house with the green-striped 25 pounder tucked proudly under his weathered arm. He ended his morning in the field by handpicking a choice watermelon, and then we'd meet under the restful shade of the broad-leafed catalpa tree to spend several hours reaping the refreshing fruits of his labor.

Every year, my grandfather, Claude Belles, grew 10-acres of Hermiston watermelons on incessantly thirsty ground in Eastern Oregon. He was a stocky built man, with thin, receding salt and pepper hair. His neck was nonexistent, making apparent his inherent bullheadedness. He was a man of few words who never raised his voice, but our communication was loud and clear in regard to our mutual love of "The King of Melons."

Grandpa would collapse into a creaky wooden lawn chair with the melon, and I would anxiously seat myself on the ground near his water-stained boots. The melon would make a familiar hollow thud when he placed it on the thick grass between us. Expertly, Grandpa slid the tip of his large razor-edged garden knife into the lush watermelon. Slowly, the melon would start splitting open length-wise, revealing its red, plumpness. So ripe, ready and filled with pure melon juice it would pop - giving way to melon chunks rocking like a laden cradle on the uncut lawn. Without fail my dust covered arms, legs and face would become dotted with splashes of pink sugary juice.

"It's perfect!" he'd say in his usual deep serious voice. We'd burst into laughter, validating Grandpa's success as a melon farmer. Then, he'd carve the fleshy, loaf-shaped heart from each watermelon half.

"One heart for you and one heart for me...no seeds!" Just before we took our first glorious bites, Grandpa would flash me a quick wink and he'd smile, revealing his babyish tooth free gums. Then we'd devour the sweet gourd of heaven using our hands for eating utensils, sticky pink juice streaming down to our elbows.

My grandfather mastered numerous trades throughout his life; in his early days he was a gambler, poker being his specialty, then he took up barbering and later he became a carpenter and a farmer. He was indeed a jack-of-all-trades, but to me he was the master of growing the sweetest, and juiciest watermelon that has ever passed my lips, even to this day.

So, Grandpa, here's to you! Every time I make this scrumptious Father's Day Fruit Salad, I am reminded of the sweltering summer afternoons we spent together swatting ants and slurping down your homegrown watermelons while sitting under the protective shade of the catalpa tree. And, Grandpa, as a special reminder of you, I always add extra big chunks of watermelon to the salad, "one heart for you and one heart for me...no seeds!"

Father's Day Fruit Salad

4 Kiwi fruit
1 mango
3 to 4 cups watermelon
3 to 4 cups honeydew
3 to 4 cups cantaloupe
2 nectarines
1 cup cherries, pitted
1 cup strawberries, halved
1 Bermuda onion, chopped fine
½ bunch fresh cilantro, chopped or shredded
3 tablespoons lemon **OR** lime juice, fresh squeezed
2 cups mild **OR** medium green salsa (also called salsa verde)

The fruits listed above are a general idea of fruits that can be used for this salad, feel free to adjust fruits to your choosing (do not use bananas, they're too soft).

Wash and de-seed all fruit. Slice fruit (fairly large pieces) into a large mixing bowl allowing the fruit to remain in layers, add onion and cilantro layers. Sprinkle with lemon **OR** lime juice and finish with green salsa. Leave the salad in layers, cover and refrigerate until it's served. Toss just before serving. Makes 8 - 2 cup servings.

To make fruit salsa: Use same fruit choices as for salad. Chop fruits and onion fine; add cilantro, lemon and green salsa. Mix all ingredients together (do not leave in layers as for salad) cover and refrigerate overnight allowing salsa to "mush-up" and flavors to meld. Serve with tortilla chips.

Recipe originates from Trish Sells, Renton, Washington, who created this recipe as a fruit salsa and Allegra Berrian, Seattle, Washington, who uses the same recipe as a fruit salad.

Chapter Three

Breads: Warm Bundles of Joy

Who doesn't love the earthy bouquet of bread fresh from the oven? Bread is indeed an unmistakable hearth and home scent that wafts through the house like coffee brewing at dawn or bacon sizzling on a hot cast iron griddle.

Home-baked bread is a family treat that's loved by all, and one I remember enjoying on the days when Mom had plenty of time to pamper the precious loaves from early morning until baking time in late afternoon. The soft thick slices framed in crispy golden crust tasted best to me when I arrived home from school and the loaves were freshly turned from the oven and resting on the cooling racks - waiting to be slathered with real country butter and homemade raspberry or apricot pineapple jam.

When you follow the Basques Sheepherder's Bread or Savory Top o' the Morning Dill Bread recipes from this chapter, I think you too will feel that successfully making bread likens to having a "bun in the oven" as it requires patience, plenty of time and most of all loving care. However *painstaking your experience in baking homemade bread, you'll be sure to find the end result is wonderful and worthwhile.*

CB

Having a Bun in the Oven

Bread is an intriguing, cross-cultural household commodity that most of us instinctively want to share. Whether we're eating tortillas, pita bread, a baguette, naan, a cinnamon raisin bagel or sourdough rolls, bread is present in all cultures and has a common language. If we break bread with peasants or with presidents, our meal would probably include some type of grain formed into a bread-like accompaniment.

Making bread from scratch, with my own two hands, is a rewarding experience. I always analogize it somewhat with pregnancy. When you're making bread (or expecting a baby), there's no way to get around the necessary process and the patience they both entail. Guesswork is ever present, and pain is usually inevitable.

Conception begins when the yeast is mixed with the sugar. It has to be done just right so the yeast (baby) can grow. The bread maker (mother) must maintain a sensitive balance between keeping the bread (baby) warm and not letting it get too cold. Adding the flour comes next, which is a guessing game (is it a girl or a boy?). No recipe is the same and everyone seems to have his or her own opinion or method.

Using good old-fashioned muscle power, the bread is then kneaded until your arms feel like they're going to fall off (labor). The dough is placed in a very large glass bowl where it doubles in girth. You've heard the term, "You can't hurry love." Well, you can't hurry bread (or a baby) either! The bread is ready for the oven when the cotton towel, draped over the bulging bundle, no longer touches the kitchen countertop.

I'm always proud of my precious creation when it comes out of the oven. And I'm sure I've been seen tenderly patting each loaf (new born) with motherly adoration.

Making homemade bread isn't all hard labor - in fact, it's a lot of fun! The first time I made this larger-than-life loaf of sheepherder's bread it reminded me of one of my favorite *I Love Lucy* television episodes when Lucy and Ethel were baking bread. A huge loaf of bread, which looked like a log, ominously emerged from the oven. Utterly stunned and speechless over their monstrous creation, the enormous loaf took on a life of its own when it slowly backed Lucy and Ethel out of the kitchen.

The Basques originally baked sheepherder's bread in an open fire pit of glowing embers, which is a method I've never been courageous enough to try. I continue using my conventional oven, a baking method that comfortably places me between building an illegal fire in my backyard and learning how to use one of those new-fangled bread-making machines.

Basques Sheepherder's Bread

> 3 cups hot tap water
> ½ cup butter
> ½ cup sugar
> 2½ teaspoons salt
> 2 packages active dry yeast
> 9 to 9 ½ cups all-purpose flour, do not sift
> Salad oil

In a bowl, combine the hot water, butter, sugar, and salt. Stir until butter melts, let cool to warm (110° to 115°). Stir in yeast, cover, and set in a warm place until bubbly, about 15 minutes. Add 5 cups of the flour and beat with a heavy-duty mixer or wooden spoon to form a thick batter. Stir in enough of the remaining flour (about 3½ cups) to form stiff dough. Turn dough out onto a floured board and knead until smooth, about 10 minutes, adding flour as needed to prevent sticking. Turn dough over in a greased bowl, cover, and let rise in a warm place until double in bulk, about 1½ hours.

Punch down dough and knead on a floured board to form a smooth ball. Cut a circle of foil to cover the bottom of the Dutch oven. Grease the inside of the Dutch oven and the underside of the lid with salad oil.

Place dough in the pot and cover with the lid. Let rise in a warm place until dough pushes up the lid by about ½", approximately 1 hour (watch closely).

Bake, covered with lid, in a 375° oven for 12 minutes. Remove lid; bake for another 30 to 35 minutes, or until loaf is golden brown and sounds hollow when tapped. Remove from oven, allow to cool for 5 minutes; turn onto a rack to cool (you'll need a helper). Makes 1 very large loaf.

Thank you to *Sunset Magazine* for giving written permission to reprint this recipe from their June 1976 issue.

Granny's Rustic Whole Wheat Bread

"You've got to try my new recipe for red onion rye bread," Mom said, excited about her "does everything for you" bread making machine.

"The bread sounds heavenly, Mom. But I won't make it because I don't want a bread machine. I think bread making is all about kneading the dough, watching it rise, punching it down, and waiting for it to rise again - the old fashioned way." I said thinking back to the days before I'd given in to using dough hoops.

"With the automatic bread maker you just dump everything into the cylinder and press the button. Presto, delicious bread every time!" Mom explained the instant-ness of the remarkable machine.

Making bread is exciting and fun for home-bakers that have patience in the kitchen. Probably getting used to using yeast and setting aside the time are two key factors in successful bread making.

Yeast alone seems to carry a mystique and can be intimidating for those who are new to making yeast breads. Keeping the liquids in the recipe below 110 degrees Fahrenheit is the only way to avoid bread that forms into a lump of warm concrete.

The investment of time in baking bread is a consideration. Bread cannot be rushed. I think that's one main reason that bread machines have become so popular – similar to crock pots, they're both quite valuable in saving time while providing savory meals.

I'm rather experimental in the kitchen and I especially enjoy making something that's tasty as well as healthful. Because of this, I've had my share of successes and failures with making bread. Homemade, or handmade artisan, bread as it's called in some bakeries, is a highly creative art form, and perhaps that's why I'm so resistant to a bread machine sitting on my countertop.

After my conversation with Mom, I couldn't resist pulling out my old "bread-bible" cookbook that I used when my kids were growing up. Wheat germ bread, granola bread, Finnish pumpernickel, millet rolls, braided soy bread, super breakfast bread, and buckwheat-honey bread were a few of the favorite breads I'd consistently make; and I added my hand-written comments in the margins. I had to chuckle at my fervor in providing proper nutrition for my kids. Could they have grown up to be anything but strapping?

Times have changed. I appreciate my mother's interest in keeping up with progress by using her bread making machine; they have a place in our instant society because they produce delicious bread. Do I cling to the old fashioned method of making bread to nurture the memory of raising my children on "bread-bible" creations?

Ring! Ring! Ring! The telephone suddenly jarred me from my thoughts.

It was Mom. "I found a recipe that's going to settle our bread making differences." She laughed knowing that our disagreement was all in fun.

"It's called Granny's Rustic Whole Wheat Bread and it's as easy as 1-2-3. It's a heavy, dark bread that's baked in 1-pound metal coffee cans - like my mother did back in the 30s."

Whether you're an old fashioned bread-making purist, a bread machine purist, or somewhere in between, this hardy whole wheat bread ensures delicious bread-making success.

Granny's Rustic Whole Wheat Bread

4 one-pound metal coffee cans, washed and dried
1 cup warm water
2 tablespoons dry yeast
½ brown sugar, packed
⅓ cup honey

⅓ cup vegetable oil
1 tablespoon salt
1 cup non-fat dry milk powder
¼ cup wheat **OR** oat bran
3 cups warm water
8 cups whole-wheat flour
4 tablespoons butter, melted

Grease coffee cans thoroughly. Mix 1-cup warm water, dry yeast, and brown sugar together in a large mixing bowl; let stand for 5 minutes. To the yeast mixture, add honey, vegetable oil, salt, dry milk powder, bran, 3-cups warm water and whole-wheat flour. Mix well. Using a large spoon, divide dough equally among the 4 cans.

Place filled coffee cans into oven on the low rack; turn oven temperature to 350° for ONE MINUTE. Turn oven OFF for 15 minutes (leave bread in oven). Turn oven back on, and set temperature at 375°. Bake 40-50 minutes or until loaves sound hollow. Remove from the oven and brush bread tops with melted butter. Allow bread to cool for 10 minutes; turn onto a cooling rack. Yields 4 loaves.

My Mean Mother

I'm delighted to share with you the following poem in prose, which is dear to my heart because of the irony in *having* a mean mother and eventually *becoming* one. This is a tribute to all mean Mothers.

The Meanest Mother in the World

"As a child, I had the meanest Mother in the world. She was real mean!

When other kids ate candy for breakfast, she made me eat cereal, or eggs and toast.

When other kids had Coke and candy for lunch, I had to eat a sandwich.

As you can guess, my dinner, too, was different from other kids.

My mother insisted on knowing were we were at all times. You'd think we were in a chain gang.

She had to know who our friends were – and what we were doing.

She insisted that if we said we'd be gone for an hour that we would be gone for one hour or less. She was really mean!

I am ashamed to admit it, but she actually had the nerve to break the child labor laws by making us work!

We had to wash dishes, make all the beds, learn to cook, and all sorts of cruel things.

I believe she lay awake nights thinking up things for us to do!

She always insisted on us telling the truth, the whole truth, and nothing but the truth.

By the time we were teenagers, she was much wiser, and our life became even more unbearable.

None of this tooting the car horn for us to come running. She embarrassed us to no end by making our dates come to the front door to get us.

I forgot to mention it, but while my friends were dating at the mature age of 12 and 13, my old-fashioned mother refused to let me date until I was 15 or 16. She was really mean!

My mother was a complete failure as a mother.

But, none of us have ever been arrested, or beaten a mate.

Each of my brothers spent time in the service of his country, willingly…no protesting.

And whom do we have to blame for this terrible way we turned out?

You're right…our mean mother!

Look at all the things we missed.

We never got to take part in a riot, never burned draft cards, or got to do a million things our friends did.

Our mean mother made us grow-up into God-fearing, educated, honest adults.

I am trying to use this as a background for raising my own children. So, I stand a little taller, and I am filled with pride when my children call me 'mean.'

You see, I'm thankful that God gave me the meanest mother in the world."

> Signed,
> Another Mother
> (Anonymous)

I'd like to pass along to you my mother's dinner roll recipe. These sweet, old-fashioned pull-apart dinner rolls are unforgettably delicious and I think you'll agree that my mean mother makes a mean dinner roll!

My Mean Mother's Dinner Rolls

½ cup water
½ cup butter or margarine
5½ to 6 cups all-purpose flour
2 packages active dry yeast
½ cup sugar
1 teaspoon salt
2 eggs, slightly beaten
¾ cup milk
¼ cup butter, melted (optional)

Heat butter and water to 110 to 120 degrees. In a large mixing bowl combine warmed butter/water mixture, ¾ cup flour, yeast, sugar, salt, eggs and milk. Gradually add remaining flour; knead about 4 minutes. Place in well-greased bowl, turning once to grease top. Cover with plastic wrap and let rise in a warm place until double in bulk.

Lightly punch dough down and divide into 12 balls, place in a 9" x 12" or 11" x 13" baking pan. *Lightly* butter a piece of plastic wrap and loosely cover rolls; place in a warm location to rise. When rolls have raised almost level to top of pan, remove plastic wrap and bake at 350° for 30 minutes or until rolls are golden brown. Remove from the oven; brush with melted butter, if desired. Cool for 5 minutes; turn onto cooling rack. Makes 12 dinner rolls.

Everybody's Irish Today

"*You can't name that baby* anything but Patrick Michael! Do you know what an honor it is to be born on St. Patrick's Day?" the head-nurse exclaimed to Mom the morning my brother came into this world.

"But, we're Norwegian, and we've decided to name him Randall Dean!" Mom insisted.

"Everyone is Irish on St. Paddy's Day!" the nurse retorted.

According to family legend, it took a bull-headed Norskie, like Mom, to stand up to the nursing staff at the hospital and give her newborn son the name my parents had chosen.

I have found those nurses' convictions - about everyone being Irish on St. Patrick's Day – to have a ring of truth because this wannabe Irish-for-a-day-woman has, throughout the years, enjoyed o' touch o' Irish luck.

One such day I found myself celebrating the green by attending an Irish potluck. What made it an Irish potluck you ask? Each person brought a green food to share, and participants were asked to incorporate green into their attire. In typical Irish fashion everyone, regardless of his or her heritage, was invited.

The serving table was a sea of green with leafy green salads, Granny Smith green apples, lime green Jell-O molds, green bean mushroom casserole, green guacamole salad, green rice cereal treats, and green pea soup, and all was nearly upstaged by a blonde Austrian man, who arrived sporting a shamrock green head of hair.

As you can imagine, a green hairdo bobbing through the crowd and good-natured bantering about who was more Irish according to the amount of green they were wearing, made for a lively get-together.

A more personal kind of "Luck of the Irish" came my way a few years ago when my then new mother-in-law, Ruthie, who is a full-blooded Swede and pushing 90 years young, presented me with a delicate treasure – a shamrock patterned Irish Belleek sugar and creamer set.

The tissue paper-thin, pale greenish-white Irish porcelain with green shamrocks lilting across its faintly waffled surface was nothing less than exquisite. An Irish doctor for whom she worked in the 1940s gave it to Ruthie, and 59 years later, she presented it to me, just after I became her daughter-in-law. I accepted the beautiful gift as a token of love welcoming me into the family. The Belleek sugar and creamer set is more valuable to me than the fabled pot o' gold at the end of the rainbow.

In recognition of Ireland's national day of celebration, why not join in the frivolity of the day by making a one-bowl, one raise dill bread. The recipe calls for cottage cheese or sour cream, which makes it a heavy, stick-to-your-ribs, moist bread that's dotted throughout with tiny green flecks of flavorful dill weed. When the leprechauns in your family catch an aromatic whiff of this delightful bread, it'll disappear faster than you can say, "Happy St. Patrick's Day!"

Savory Top o' the Morning Dill Bread

¼ cup warm tap water
1 package dry yeast
3½ cups all-purpose flour, divided
3 tablespoons granulated sugar or honey
½ teaspoon soda
1 teaspoon salt
2 level teaspoons dried dill weed
1 cup cottage cheese **OR** sour cream
2 eggs
1¼ cups all-purpose flour

Place water in large mixing bowl, sprinkle with yeast, and stir using a wire whip. Allow yeast to soften for 3-5 minutes.

To yeast/water mixture, add 3½ cups flour, sugar, soda, salt, dill weed, cottage cheese **OR** sour cream, and eggs. Mix with a high-speed, heavy-duty mixer until smooth.

63

*With mixer on low-medium speed, gradually add 1¼ cup flour. When flour is fully absorbed, increase speed and knead on high-speed for 2 minutes.

Spray a large loaf pan with non-stick cooking spray. Gently press bread dough into pan covering bottom and corners; spray top with non-stick cooking spray and cover loosely with plastic wrap. Place in a warm area, allow bread to rise for 40-60 minutes or until dough has risen level to top of loaf pan.

Bake at 350 for 15 minutes; reduce heat to 325° and bake for additional 15 minutes. Remove bread from oven, cool in upright position for 5 minutes; turn out on cooling rack. Slice bread when it's cool enough to handle and slather with fresh butter. Savory Top o' the Morning Dill Bread is also delicious when it's just popped-up from the toaster. Yields: 1 loaf bread, approximately 12 slices.

* This is very stiff, heavy bread dough and it's easier to make using a heavier mix master, preferably with dough hoops. If you'd prefer to make it using a hand mixer, follow the recipe directions to the *, at which time turn the dough onto a floured board and work the last 1¼ cups flour into the dough by hand. Rise in warm place and bake according to recipe directions.

Chapter Four

Enter the Entrées

Main dishes take center stage at every meal regardless of how elegant or casual the occasion might be. For me, it's fun to think of an entrée as an edible centerpiece. With this mind-set, I'm more inclined to create an enticing main dish and presentation that will garner oos and ahs from my dinner guests.

Chapter Four offers a selection of entrée recipes that will nourish any cook's creative expression. The featured recipes are suitable for assorted dining affairs and begins with Parmesan Meatloaf and Roasted Garlic Potatoes - both are 1950s comfort food staples. My Aunt Joy's Shrimp Casserole meets us mid-way through the chapter, which is an absolutely succulent from-microwave-to-table-in-minutes entrée that's sure to trick your taste buds into thinking you're eating gourmet. Enter the Entrées closes with a light-hearted Chicken Trilogy.

CB

Cynthia Briggs

Meatloaf ~ The Comfort food

"So, what time's dinner?" asked the clerk at Petrich's Market as she tallied up the items in our grocery cart. She wore an eager smile and Maggie was boldly stamped on her black plastic nametag. "It looks like you're having meatloaf for dinner. It's one of my favorites - what folks nowadays call comfort food, Maggie said, as she handed my husband, Ed, his change.

"When I was a kid, my mother made meatloaf on rainy days, and she made macaroni and tomatoes whenever she was late getting home from bridge club," Maggie continued. "Meatloaf or macaroni and tomatoes makes me think back to the security of my childhood." Maggie crossed her arms and leaned against the cash register.

"Oh, yes, a thunder storm always puts me in the mood for a home cooked meal," I responded. Ed and I smiled at each other enjoying Maggie's cheerful prattle. We considered buying another pound of ground round and more potatoes just in case Maggie showed up at my mother-in-law's door at dinnertime.

"Enjoy your supper. I hope you beat the next storm home," Maggie's voice was soft. As she turned away from us I could see the lines in her face had softened noticeably. Her eyes were as misty as the green pasture that surrounded the rural market.

The sky had cleared, at least for the time being, so we took a different route back home to capture glimpses of the pastoral countryside on film. Maggie's mention of macaroni and tomatoes lingered with me and I began thinking about comfort food. I'd never heard of macaroni and tomatoes before and I had serious doubts about the concoction. Perhaps, there were spices, or something more interesting in it that Maggie hadn't divulged.

I wondered, "Does macaroni and tomatoes taste delicious to Maggie or is it the memories she savors?"

Surprise Parmesan Meatloaf

1½ pounds lean ground beef
1 cup soft breadcrumbs
¾ cup milk
½ cup dry onion, chopped
½ cup Parmesan cheese, finely grated
1 egg, slightly beaten
1 teaspoons salt
¼ teaspoon pepper
1 heaping teaspoon oregano leaves
½ cup thick barbecue sauce

Heat oven to 350°. Combine all ingredients except barbecue sauce; mix lightly. Fold into a greased 5" x 9" x 3" loaf pan. Gently press to remove large bubbles. Bake at 350°for 30 minutes. Using a baster, remove any grease that has formed in the bottom of pan. Spread with half the barbecue sauce and bake 15 minutes; top with remaining barbecue sauce, bake another 15 minutes. Serve sprinkled with additional Parmesan cheese and barbecue sauce on the side. Make 6 servings.

Roasted Garlic Potatoes

5 medium baking potatoes cut in half-length wise, score on cut surface
2 tablespoons butter, melted
½ teaspoon garlic powder
½ teaspoon paprika
Dash of salt

Mix together melted butter, garlic powder, paprika and salt. Pour into a 13" x 9" x 2" baking pan. For uniform crispness, coat the entire bottom of the pan with the melted butter. Place potatoes in the pan, scored surface in the butter. Bake at 350°, uncovered for 35 to 40 minutes or until scored side is crispy and brown. Makes 6 servings.

Fighting the Battle of the Bulge

"Well, we're headed into another battle. This time we'll call it WWII." Ed said, as he turned into the United Methodist Church parking lot.

"Honey, it's not like we're about to face a firing squad." I couldn't help but be amused with his flair toward the dramatic. "Maybe after a few Weight Watchers meetings, we'll get back into the swing of dieting," I said, trying to look at the bright side of our on-going battle of the bulge.

Last year, Ed lost 56 pounds and I lost 18 (56 and 18 is not a misprint) on the Weight Watchers program. It was challenging to stick with a diet that didn't include ice cream as one of the major food groups. But we managed nicely on the plan for over a year.

When we decided to move to Carlsbad, we started bouncing off the WWI wagon. In a nutshell, we've spent the last 4-months grazing our way south. Every evening over dessert we promised each other that we'd begin WWII the moment we set foot in New Mexico. Here we are, 23 and 18 pounds heavier, pulling up our bootstraps in the church parking lot – preparing for WWII.

During WWI we learned the rewards of exchanging one *bad* food for a *good* one. It's basically a food item trade-off that works well most of the time. However, some suggested exchanges are ludicrous, such as drinking a glass of sugar-free lemonade to satisfy a craving for chocolate cake. They had to be kidding! Next, I suppose someone will try to convince us that fat-free cottage cheese is a succulent prime rib dinner or that jicama sticks are maple bars.

Our desire to fight the battle of the bulge has prompted us into seeking out and experimenting with new and alternative foods. Quaker Crispy Caramel Corn rice snacks are a perfect example. I've started purchasing these sweet, crispy discs by the case and I store them in my car for on-the-go snack attacks. When our taste buds scream, "Give me sodium!" Lay's WOW chips calm the little beasts. Nature's Own Light Bread allows us to enjoy a BLT. We've even resorted to using I Can't Believe It's Not Butter, Zero Calories because it tastes better than simply waving the butter above the toast.

We earned our good conduct medals about 6 months into WWI, but only after we'd faced compromising situations head-on. At the first meeting it was impressed upon us, by our fellow comrades, that munching on pizza during the meeting was not acceptable behavior. Six weeks later, forgetting the earlier pizza incident, Ed stood up and asked, "How about we all go for Mexican food after the meeting?" Everyone in the room joined us and we had the time of our life. However, the following week the drill sergeant (oops, I mean WWI instructor) took us aside and pointed out the potential physical dangers of mentioning pizza *or* Mexican food in a room full of ravenous people who aren't related to Twiggy. We can only surmise that Ed caught them on a good night.

Now that we've re-upped for a second stint, we're trying to do everything right. We religiously study our weight loss books. I've pulled out my low-*everything* recipes, including my favorite legal meal, Chicken Enchilada Casserole. I've stocked the refrigerator with 5 pounds of fresh broccoli and a quart of non-fat ranch dip. The treadmill (ugh!) stands ready for duty 24 hours a day.

How did we do the first week of WWII? It was a victory, Ed lost 8 pounds and I lost 1 (8 and 1 is not a misprint). Morale is running high among the troops. But I'm wondering if the esprit de corps will sustain itself when my husband is caught whispering into his cell phone, "Hello, I'd like to order a pepperoni pizza to go…"

Chicken Enchilada Casserole

½ cup onion, chopped
2 garlic cloves, minced
1½ cups canned Mexican tomatoes, do not drain

½ cup mushrooms, sliced
½ cup green chiles, roasted, peeled and diced
1 teaspoon salt
¼ teaspoon pepper
8 ounces lean chicken breast, cooked and chopped
    fine
4 corn tortillas (6" size)
4 ounces low-fat Colby & Monterey Jack cheese,
    shredded
1 - 4 ounce can sliced olives, drained
½ cup fat-free sour cream **OR** ½ cup plain yogurt
½ cup cilantro, chopped

Spray a large, nonstick skillet with cooking spray. Lightly brown onion and garlic in prepared skillet over medium-high heat. Add tomatoes (including liquid), mushrooms, chiles and seasonings. Simmer, uncovered, for 8 to 10 minutes over medium heat until sauce begins to thicken.

Transfer half the tomato mixture to a medium bowl; add the chopped chicken; stir and set aside. Remove remaining tomato mixture from the stovetop and set aside.

Preheat oven to 400°. Spray an oblong-baking dish with nonstick cooking spray and set aside. Using a dry, cast iron skillet, heat 1 tortilla on both sides (about 30 seconds on each side) just until it begins to soften. Lay the tortilla flat and add ¼ ounce cheese and ¼ the chicken mixture. Roll stuffed tortilla up and place in prepared baking dish with the seam side down. Repeat process until all tortillas are filled.

Pour reserved tomato mixture over enchiladas, top with remaining cheese; and bake until cheese melts, 15 minutes. Garnish with sliced olives, fat-free sour cream and chopped cilantro.

Serves 4 light appetites. Weight Watchers = 3 points per serving or 261 calories per serving

Crazy Mixed-up Zucchini

"Not in my lifetime!" my husband commented the first time I mentioned having zucchini for dinner.

A few days later I created my finest blend of Crazy Mixed-up Zucchini. He didn't know he'd eaten squash until he peeked into the skillet for a second helping. "Is this stir-fry?" he asked me, peering at "it" suspiciously over the top of his glasses.

"Yes, 'it's' chicken stir-fry…Italian style." I replied smugly. At that moment my recipe for Crazy Mixed-up Zucchini was re-named Italian Chicken Stir-Fry. You've heard the term "it's all in a name?" It seems to apply in this case because it's now one of Hubby's favorites.

I have to admit it took me a few years to master the art of cooking summer squash. The first year that I grew zucco (gourd in Italian), I experienced nightmares about the vigorous vines first overtaking the garden, then the house and ultimately all three barns. By mid-summer of the third growing season, reality told me that zucchini is one of the most prolific vegetables known to man. However, I was determined to make the best use of every squash the plants could bear.

One day, as luck would have it, I came across a recipe for Mock Pea Soup. "No one will ever know that it's really zucchini soup," I connived. My kitchen was a virtual hub of steaming, stirring and whirring. I canned more soup that summer than I could find jars to fill and by September everyone in the family shuddered at the mere sight of the stuff.

Another attempt to be creative with the courgette (a common European term for the young zucchini) was to make zucchini bread. Most of us know that zucchini bread is delicious, but how much of it can one family eat? One interesting variation of zucchini bread, called for replacing half the zucchini in the recipe with grated carrots for a confetti effect. Heaven only knows we welcomed the variety. But one problem still remained…it didn't use-up enough zucchini!

There were summers when I barely crawled out from under the mound of zucchini, but I did learn that longevity, hardiness and versatility are some of the inherent traits of summer squash.

Archaeologists have found evidence of the small-seed varieties of the green gourd being cultivated in Mexico around 7000-5000 BC. The Pilgrims (a hardy-breed themselves) boiled and baked summer squash, upon their arrival at Plymouth Rock. They called it squash from its Native American name – askootasquash.

A friend, obviously not aware of the gourd's distinguished lineage, expressed his disgust for the vegetable, "Zucchini will grow from cracks in concrete, and it doesn't need soil, water or nurturing!" However, when he thought no one was looking, I saw him dipping raw, thinly sliced zucco into ranch dressing...more than once. So, if your green thumb is really black, you can throw some squash seeds at a clump of dirt and become a master gardener overnight.

Zucchini is not going away any time soon. So, perhaps we should appreciate the advantages it has to offer. It's easy to grow, versatile in recipes and is a natural "Good Samaritan" to us all. Eaten with the skin on, green summer squash is packed with vitamin A. It'll shore up your immune system and help your skin, hair, teeth and gums flourish. All we have to do is eat it!

I'm not sure if people will ever recognize the merits of the much-maligned summer squash. However, everyone will sit up and take notice when newspaper headlines declare:

EXTRA!
EXTRA!
ZUCCHINI
TAKES
OVER
THE
WORLD!

Italian Chicken Stir-Fry

1 large chicken breast, sliced into ½" x 2" strips
1 to 2 garlic cloves, chopped fine
¼ cup olive oil
4 to 5 small green zucchini squash; scrub (do not peel) and cut into ⅛" thick slices
1 to 2 small yellow crook-necked squash; scrub (do not peel) & cut into ⅛" thick slices
1 large Walla Walla sweet onion, quartered and sliced
5 large fresh mushrooms, sliced
4 to 5 cups tomatoes, stewed Italian
1 tablespoon dried oregano
1 teaspoon dried basil
8 ounces medium size pasta shells, cooked and drained
½ cup Parmesan cheese, finely grated
½ cup Parmesan cheese, coarsely grated
Freshly ground pepper

Heat oil in a large, deep skillet over medium-high burner. Cook chicken and garlic in oil until lightly browned. Push to sides of pan. Add green and yellow squash, onion, and mushrooms; stir and fry until some of the vegetables begin to brown (do not overcook). Add tomatoes (including liquid), oregano, and basil. Cover and simmer for about 15 to 20 minutes; stirring frequently.

Vegetables should be hot all the way through but still firm. Remove from heat. Stir in finely grated Parmesan cheese and cooked pasta. Garnish with coarsely grated Parmesan cheese and ground pepper. Add a loaf of crusty garlic bread and a glass of Chardonnay and you'll have all you need for a delightful summertime meal. Makes 4 generous servings.

Suggestions: Summer squash cooks very quickly. The key to success with cooking it is to sear it quickly over moderately high heat and use plenty of seasonings. Variations: pork, veal or Italian sausage can be used instead of chicken. Celery, green and/or red bell pepper, corn, peas, or any favorite vegetable can be added to suit your personal taste. For a lighter flavor, 3 tablespoons fresh, oregano and 1 tablespoon fresh basil (both chopped fine) can be substituted for the dried herbs. Garnish with crushed red peppers to add some real pizzazz!

How about some Brew with your Sauerbraten?

"We'll be back in 2 hours - just in time for that sauerbraten dinner you promised us!" Dad said as his long legs carried him swiftly across the front yard toward his pick-up truck. His friend, Pat, was waiting in the truck leisurely puffing on his pipe. They were going on an afternoon adventure to scope out a piece of ground as they did so often when Dad was preparing to build another house.

"That's perfect timing! While you're gone, Mom and I are going to do some prep work for our friend, Cheryl's baby shower and bottle a batch of Christmas beer," I shouted to Dad from my back porch as he closed the truck door behind him and waved a hasty goodbye.

When I went back into the house, I could see that Mom had finished washing the brown 1-quart beer bottles. We started arranging the empties on the floor in a half-circle in front of the weathered 10-gallon crock, which Pat and Dad had hoisted onto a chair for us so it would be easier to siphon every sparkling drop from the crock into the bottles.

"You know, for two people who don't drink beer, we certainly spend a lot of time bottling hooch!" Mom smiled. She was ribbing me and I knew that she also enjoyed the challenge of making homebrew, because much like wine, the finished product turned out different every year.

"It's worth all the fuss to see my beer-loving friends' faces light up at Christmas when I hand them a bottle of pure golden, bubbly brew, made right here in my own dining room!" I replied peering down into the crock. We listened for the beer's familiar "hiss, sizzle, gurgle," that we had heard earlier in the week, it was quiet and still, a temporary flatness, which indicated it was ready to bottle.

We each grabbed a siphoning tube and pulled up a chair. We dipped one end of the tube into the crock, sucked on the other end of the tube to start the brew flowing through the tube and began siphoning fresh green beer into our 72 bottles.

We no sooner got started when, "Ring! Ring!" I removed my siphon hose from the crock and laid it aside to answer the phone. Throughout the afternoon we had numerous calls, which meant we had to start a new tap with each interruption.

The phone rang again just as we were filling the last few bottles. "Eello! Oh hi, Cheerryl. I'm so gla...at you called. Ows our expectant Mommy do'in?" I said into the phone.

Mom tapped me on the shoulder and whispered, "Remind her that we need a final guest lissht."

"Do ya think we should start cap'in some of these bo...ttles?" Mom asked, pulling the bottle capper to the edge of the dining room table and through several pools of spilled beer, which had dribbled down the table leg splashing onto the floor.

"That's a go...oot idea, Moon, the crock is mtee."

I glanced out the dining room window, "Oh my gaawsh! Pad and Dat are comm'n up the driveway! Is it dinnertime all ratty?"

Mom started tittering and pointed an inebriated finger at me, "I think yur tiptssy!"

We looked at each other with a wavering glance, and realized that we were both feeling the effects of the beer. Suddenly everything was funny! We couldn't stop giggling, our faces quickly covered with tears of laughter.

Much to Dad and Pat's surprise, they found Mom and me surrounded by a sea of beer bottles, reeking of brewski, and three sheets to the wind.

"Hey, Pat, get a load of these two teetotalers - they've got a snoot full!" Dad cried out above the clamor, and then both men burst into laughter.

Dad and Pat were good sports about our unintentional toot. With the help of our slurred instructions, the men boiled some red potatoes and put the finishing touches on the sauerbraten. It seemed especially tasty that merry fall afternoon.

Although I haven't made beer for a while, I often make sauerbraten when the weather turns cold and blustery. Sauerbraten is an inexpensive cut of beef, which is marinated for several days in vinegar brine, then slowly roasted until tender, and smothered in a rich blend of tangy sour cream and spices just before serving. This is a hearty, fail-proof German entrée that hits the spot whether you're serving it with or without homebrew.

Oktoberfest Sauerbraten

1 large arm cut chuck roast
2 medium onions, sliced
1 lemon, sliced
1½ cups red wine vinegar
2½ cup water
12 whole cloves
6 bay leaves
12 whole black peppercorns
1 tablespoon salt
1 tablespoon granulated sugar
¼ teaspoon ground ginger
2 to 4 tablespoons cooking oil
1 pint sour cream

Place roast in a large, glass baking dish. Prepare marinade in a large bowl (a mixing bowl with a pour spout works well) by combining onions, lemon, vinegar, water, cloves, bay leaves, peppercorns, salt, sugar and ginger; stir well. Pour marinade over roast and cover. Marinate roast in refrigerator for 3 to 4 days, turning at least twice daily.

Set oven at 300°. Remove roast from marinade, reserving all remaining marinade except for the lemons, which should be discarded. Using paper towels, dry the roast thoroughly and set aside.

Pour cooking oil into a large heated skillet and brown roast on both sides. Place roast in a large baking pan or roaster, that's been treated with cooking spray, pour marinade over roast; cover.

Bake for 3 hours, or until tender. Move roast to a serving platter, and keep it warm in the oven while sauce is being prepared. Remove and discard bay leaves, cloves and peppercorns from pan juices. Pour juice into a saucepan, bring it to a boil, and remove from the heat; stir in sour cream.

Boiled red potatoes and slow-cooked green beans or steamed cabbage make an excellent accompaniment for sauerbraten.

Makes 6 to 8 generous servings.

Aunt Joy helps recall Childhood Memories

"It's impossible that you've been married 47 years!" I cried out over the phone. I called Aunt Joy, who lives in San Diego, to thank her for a delicious shrimp casserole recipe she recently shared with me and the conversation generated sweet memories of the 1950s.

Joy tempered a laugh. Her slow, husky modulation conveyed a soothing tone that is so familiar to my dad's side of the family. "It's astonishing to me too that the years have passed so quickly," she said. "It seems like yesterday when Jack and I eloped to Idaho and your Aunt Gloria surprised us with a wedding cake she'd whipped up in Mama's kitchen."

"Were you the bride Uncle Tony and Uncle Ken pushed down Main Street in a wheel barrel?" I asked.

"Yes, they took me on a ride through town in a wheel barrel; it was my brothers' version of a wedding announcement. They reveled in capturing a new bride, then racing through the streets with her squealing and making a fuss.

"The day my brothers whisked me away for the wheel barrel soiree, we took a detour through the feed store where Daddy was purchasing chicken feed. They wheeled me right past him and he didn't even look up!" Joy was fully appreciating that September 29, back in 1953.

"Your granddad had such a dry wit! I'll never know whether he was ignoring our antics, or if he really didn't hear the ruckus!" I could tell from the warmth in her voice that she was smiling.

I was 7 when Jack and Joy were courting, and I was totally committed to being their number one pest. Every afternoon Jack drove Joy home from school, and when I saw his gray sedan come barreling up the long, dusty driveway I'd run and hide on the backside of the shingled house. Hunkered down near the heady, pale pink peonies that my grandmother was so adept at cultivating, I'd wait until the dust, and the silence, settled around their car.

When the two lovebirds were in the middle of their predictably long goodbye, I'd sneak up onto the wide, rubberized running board, "Ha, ha! I see you...you're smooching!" I'd repetitiously chirp at them in an obnoxious childish tune.

With a furrowed brow and crimson face, Joy would demand, "Go away! Leave us alone you silly kid!"

"I'm gonna tell Gramma...I'm gonna tell Grandpa, I'd sing bouncing up and down gleefully."

"Will you go away if I give you a nickel?" Jack bribed.

Placing my hand firmly on my hip and with my lower jaw sticking out as far as it would go, I'd holler smartly, "I wanna see it first to make sure it's real!" as if I would have known a fake nickel from the real thing.

"Oh, here it is! Will this get rid of you?" Jack smiled, showing his perfectly straight, white teeth; and knowing the next day we'd be going through the same ritual.

Calling my aunt was a gentle reminder of how time finds a home between the many folds of our lives. It's an inevitable journey, which for most of us moves swiftly and silently through the vestibule of life.

It's pleasing to me that an elegant shrimp casserole recipe was the impetus for re-connecting with my aunt; and much like the savory memories of my childhood, this recipe is delightful.

Aunt Joy's Shrimp Casserole

1½ pounds fresh or frozen uncooked medium shrimp
   (21-31 count),
peeled with tails removed
¼ to ½ stick butter
4 garlic cloves, pressed
5 small zucchini (about 6" to 7" long) cut into ¼"
   slices

2 tablespoons onion, chopped
2 to 3 medium tomatoes, chopped
1 to 1½ cups Parmesan cheese, freshly grated
Salt and freshly ground pepper to taste

Place butter and garlic in a 2½ - 3-quart glass casserole dish, microwave until butter has melted. Layer shrimp, zucchini, onion, and tomatoes over butter/garlic mixture and top with Parmesan cheese. Cover, microwave on high for 10 to 15 minutes, or until zucchini slices are tender and shrimp are pink. Add salt and pepper to taste and serve with hot rice. Makes 4-6 servings.

Note: Uncooked shrimp are gray when they're purchased - not pink, and they're used in this recipe to avoid over-cooking.

Recipe comes from the kitchen of Joy Ann Pape, San Diego, California.

Going Whole-Hog for Spare Ribs

"Oink, oink, oink!" two, wiry 15-pound piglets curiously grunted from the inside of a wiggling gunnysack. The bristly weaners originally descended from Yorkshire, England where they were called Large White swine, but we named them Pork and Beans, brother and sister from the same litter. They were the first livestock that we added to our tiny, 3-acre farm in Auburn, Washington.

Pork was raised strictly to fill our deep freeze, and ultimately our dinner plates. He served that purpose with fine distinction when he reached 6 months old and 250 pounds.

We kept Beans for breeding, so we could sell her offspring to help offset the cost of raising livestock. Beans was curiously docile, surprisingly intelligent and extremely social. "Sniff, snort, blow, snort, puff, snort," she'd grunt, while wallowing in the fresh sawdust that lined her pen. She loved to have her belly scratched with an iron garden rake. To get our attention, she'd gently nudge our heels with her snout and gleefully roll over onto her side. Her long throaty grunts said, "Ah, thank you, that feels so good!"

Occasionally, Beans would escape from her well-shored pen. I'd breathlessly chase her down the road, through the neighbor's milk barn, and over cattle-dotted pastures. Her stout legs swiftly carried her over the countryside, while I ran behind her, waving a switch and yelling, "You blasted pig, go back to your pen!" I'm sure there were days when the foray provided morning coffee entertainment for neighboring farmers.

Eventually, I realized that Beans was inadvertently escaping from her pen. Thereafter, when I saw her lumbering down the driveway on the loose, I'd simply hit my switch along side the house and scream, "Beans go home!" She'd make a speedy, and amazingly agile, hairpin turn back to her pen.

There were other times that Beans stirred up a commotion. One morning, my 5-year-old son came screaming into the house, "Mom, come quick! Beans is hurt...bad! She has blood all over her head!"

I raced to the barn expecting the worst. Thankfully, no harm had come to the pampered pig. The day before a local farmer generously gave me a wheel-barrel full of crisp beets for pig fodder. I filled her trough with the beets and left her to root through the welcome bounty. Beans feasted on the plump reddish-purple beets. Consequently, she was blood red from her snout to mid-belly.

We only heard the pitter-patter of piglet hooves twice during Bean's 3-year reign on the farm. Unfortunately, it's a farm fact-of-life that livestock have to pull their own weight. We were sad when she had to leave us.

She made a grand exit by tipping the scale at a whopping 500 pounds. Beans was the single farm animal that captured our hearts and the only head of livestock that went into someone else's deep freeze.

Helen's Oven Barbecued Spare Ribs

1½ to 2 pounds, fresh, lean pork spare ribs
¼ cup brown sugar
1 tablespoon chili powder
1 teaspoon each salt, paprika and celery seed
½ cup cider vinegar
1 (10 ¾ oz can) condensed tomato soup

Set oven on broil. Mix brown sugar, chili powder, salt, paprika and celery seed together in a medium sized bowl. Place ribs (lean side up) in a large, foil-lined baking pan. Sprinkle half the sugar and spice mixture onto the ribs. Broil ribs until mixture begins to bubble, about 10 minutes (watch closely because sugar mixture burns easily). Turn ribs; sprinkle with remaining sugar and spice mixture; broil until sugar bubbles.

Set oven at 350°. Whisk vinegar and soup together in a medium sized bowl; pour vinegar and soup mixture over ribs. Cover and bake for 45 minutes, remove cover and bake, uncovered, for additional 45 minutes, basting occasionally. Serve with mashed potatoes, corn on the cob and steamed broccoli. Makes 4 servings.

This recipe comes from the kitchen of the late Helen Robertson, Seattle, Washington.

"The Chicken Trilogy"
Part One of Three

"Gramma! He got me! He pecked me again!" I sobbed as I threw my arms around my grandmother's legs and buried my tear stained face into her apron. The barnyard bully had once again forced me to seek Gramma's protection.

I was a mere 4 years old when Gramma assigned me the daily task of gathering eggs from the hen house. Gramma knew that I delighted in slipping the eggs from beneath the hens' warm fluffy tail feathers. Sometimes I'd disturb the girls and they'd fly from their straw lined nest squawking in protest. But, over all they were patient with my innocent awkwardness. In contrast, the hen house rooster had a zero tolerance policy with me setting foot into his territory. The foul bird had given me good reason to be terrified of him and he'd turned my favorite farm chore into a daytime nightmare.

Every day I'd scamper to the hen house to collect the eggs with renewed hope that the vicious creature had gotten lost during the night and couldn't find his way back to the barnyard. But, without fail, he'd fly at me with his angry claws, flapping his powerful wings and sweeping sand into my eyes. He'd knock me to the ground and peck me repeatedly with his wickedly sharp beak.

Gramma's presence alone was usually intimidating because she tipped the scale at 250 pounds and stood 5' 10" tall. Using her size and a crusty glare, she attempted some mediating tactics with the out-of-control rooster by standing guard at the chicken yard gate while I collected the eggs. She brandished a rubber garden-hose club with the chopping block ominously looming in the background.

I'm not sure if the rooster was just plain stupid or if he underestimated Gramma's experience at wielding a cleaver. But, the day came when he found out who ruled the roost.

"That bird has gotten too big for his breeches! He's pecked you for the last time!" She picked me up and set me out of her path.

"Where's my hatchet?" she asked. The wooden screen door slammed behind her with a worn-out, "bang...flop...flop!" Gramma advanced toward the chicken yard like a female bear protecting her young. Her amazingly smooth momentum was uninterrupted as she swiftly grabbed her hatchet from the chopping stump.

I started giggling when Gramma charged past the hen house with her sights on the overly zealous rooster. The feathers flew and yet another notch was carved into the chopping block. Gramma had put the ferocious fowl in his place for good.

After plucking the last of the rooster's pinfeathers, Gramma plunged the tough old bird into the stew pot. I couldn't stop giggling.

At dinner that evening I grinned fiendishly and cackled with guilt-free satisfaction when Gramma served Chicken Broccoli Soufflé. It was comforting for me to know that I'd be able to gather eggs in peace and never again be terrorized by that ornery rooster.

Never Fail Chicken Broccoli Soufflé

6 large, fresh eggs, separated
1 cup sharp cheese, grated
1 (10 ounce can) condensed cream of celery soup
10 ounces milk
½ teaspoon dry mustard
¼ teaspoon sea salt
¼ teaspoon white pepper, freshly ground
1½ cups broccoli (or mushrooms, celery, onions, peas), chopped

1 cup chicken (or shrimp, crab, ham, smoked salmon), cooked and diced

Beat egg yolks together in a large bowl. Mix soup into egg yolks, then add milk, salt, dry mustard, and pepper. In a separate large bowl, whip the egg whites until stiff peaks form. Gently fold the egg yolk mixture into the egg whites. Continue folding in meat, vegetables and cheese.

Fold into an un-greased, 1½ quart soufflé dish. Bake, uncovered, 350°, for 45 minutes or until a knife inserted into the center comes out clean. Serve immediately. Makes 4 servings

This recipe comes from the kitchen of Pat Rowan, Maple Valley, Washington.

"The Chicken Trilogy" Part Two of Three

"Betty, here's my recipe for Easy Oven Fried Chicken that you wanted," Lucille said to her neighbor. "Speaking of chicken, are those your chickens running around loose in my backyard?" She slipped the recipe in her pocket and the two women hastened toward the sliding glass door to get a better look.

"No, they're not my hens. We clipped their wings and repaired the chicken yard fence yesterday."

Betty wiped the steam from the glass and peered outside into the early evening darkness. The rain was pelting down in heavy torrents. Lucille's backyard had become a pool of wet grass. A flurry of Rhode Island Red hens were scurrying about in the yard, flapping their water soaked wings against drenching rain. "Oh my gosh! Those are my hens! We've got to get them back into a dry pen before they catch pneumonia."

Lucille quickly followed Betty out into the weather to corral the feathered escapees.

"Here, Lucille, these salmon fishing nets will make catching them much easier," Betty shouted as she shoved a huge net in Lucille's direction.

Betty and Lucille chased the squawking chickens through several neighboring yards. The hens noisily dodged swooping nets as the two determined women splashed their way down the usually quiet rural street. Overly excited, the birds bolted through an overgrown cow pasture where Betty slipped and rolled across the grass and Lucille slid through a puddle of muck netting a fence post instead of a hen. Customers at a nearby Arco Mini-Mart watched in disbelief as the net carrying duo chased the fluttering flock past the gas pumps and then disappeared into the squall.

"Enough is enough!" Betty told Lucille. "Let's go back home and get dried out. Look at us - we're soaked! Those birds have no intention of being rounded up tonight."

"You won't get an argument out of me," Lucille replied. "But, before we change our clothes, let's check the chicken coop and see how they managed to break free."

Chuckling, Lucille added. "Maybe we'll get lucky and find that some of them went back to the pen on their own. Then we won't be going back completely empty-handed."

Betty's eyes were flat. She was too tired, wet, muddy and frustrated to find any humor in the situation.

There were no visible signs of damage to the outer fencing around the chicken yard. Other than being soaked from the downpour, everything appeared to be in place. "How did the chickens escape?" they wondered.

Betty opened the hen house door. A single light bulb that dangled from the ceiling swayed gently, making it possible for them to see inside the room. Lucille peeked in over Betty's shoulder.

The room was dry, warm and undisturbed. The hens were all huddled together on their roost. They had been in bed for the night and safe from the storm since dusk.

The chickens looked up at the two astonished women, softly clucking as if to ask, "Why are you disturbing us at this time of the night?"

"Betty, we're chicken rustlers!" Lucille shrieked. "The chickens we were trying to net must belong to Mr. Brown who lives down by the school."

"I feel so stupid!" Betty started laughing. She was embarrassed but relieved to know her laying hens were out of harms way.

Lucille pulled a sopping wet recipe from her pocket and handed it to Betty, "Why don't you go home and try this chicken recipe...it's far tastier than eating crow!"

Easy Oven Fried Chicken

1 frying chicken, cut-up
1 stick margarine or butter
2 cups flour
¼ teaspoon paprika
1 teaspoon sea salt
¼ teaspoon pepper, freshly ground

Heat oven to 350°. Put the margarine in a large, aluminum foil lined, baking pan with sides, such as a heavy-duty jellyroll pan. Place the pan in the oven so the butter will melt, covering the bottom of the pan. Rinse the chicken pieces and dry thoroughly on paper towels; set aside.

Combine flour, paprika, salt and pepper. Dredge chicken in flour mixture. Shake excess flour from the chicken pieces and place them in the pan over the melted margarine. For best results, arrange the chicken so pieces aren't touching. Bake for 30 minutes, uncovered, then turn chicken pieces and bake for another 30 minutes, uncovered. If desired, continue baking and turning the chicken (in 10 minute intervals) to achieve desired crispness. Makes 4 servings.

"The Chicken Trilogy"
Part Three of Three

Bobbi peeked through the wooden slats of the backyard gate. She crossed her legs and wiggled. The outhouse was in clear view. "Where's Felicity? She's a mean old chicken!" Bobbi muttered.

Tiny and petite for her 6 years, she felt utterly defenseless against the cranky bird. Didn't the chicken understand that when nature called she had to walk the path to the outhouse?

Bobbi was puzzled because Mommy, Daddy, Grandma or Grandpa wouldn't help her. They just kept saying, "Honey, you've got to learn to defend yourself!"

Bobbi made every effort to avoid Felicity. She'd watch closely, from inside the gate to make sure the chicken wasn't in sight, with her eyes fixed on the outhouse door, she'd quickly open the gate and make a run for the privy. The bird would suddenly jump from behind a nearby woodpile batting Bobbi with her swift wings. Bobbi thought that perhaps the gate noise was alerting the insensitive creature. So, she left the gate standing open and patiently waited for signs of Felicity. With the chicken out of sight and a clear footpath, Bobbi sprinted up the trail, only to be blocked again by the persistent fowl! Then there were times when the sly bird would let Bobbi go to the outhouse only to ambush her upon the return trip.

"Does Felicity ever sleep?" Bobbi wondered. Morning, noon and night the crotchety fowl menaced her. In Bobbi's more desperate moments, with no hope of eluding the chicken, Bobbi resorted to squatting in the yard, only to be caught and scolded by her mother. Consequently, trying to out-wait the bird didn't work either. Her guess was that the hen's bladder was bigger, better and stronger.

"Bobbi, you've got to show the chicken whose boss," Dad reminded her. "Stand up for yourself. No one else is going to."

"But, Daddy, I'm afraid of her!" Bobbi cried hopelessly. The old bird continued to get the best of Bobbi. And to make matters worse all the grownups were on the chicken's side!

One morning Bobbi woke up feeling grumpy. She was fed-up with having to grapple with the chicken.

"Leave me alone, I have to go potty!" Bobbi barked at her mother as she marched outside. Her blond curls bounced off her shoulders and her short, determined legs carried her toward the outdoor facilities.

Predictably, Felicity leaped from behind a bale of straw. She lunged at Bobbi and arched her neck, threatening Bobbi with her sharp beak.

At that moment something snapped in Bobbi. The chicken had bullied her for the last time.

With her hands on her hips, she bent down and faced the chicken head-on. Bobbi waved her arms and hands in a mad frenzy and bellowed like a banshee as she squared-off, nose to beak, with the flabbergasted hen.

"Squawk! Squawk! Squawk!" Felicity protested.

A scuffle ensued. Needless to say, thereafter, Felicity gave Bobbi a wide path, including the one to the outhouse.

Bobbi learned the importance of sticking up for herself. But she also discovered the benefits of coming to a sweet understanding with someone who has a sour disposition.

Sweet & Sour Chicken

1 cutup fryer **OR** 5 chicken breasts
8 ounces Russian or Catalina salad dressing
1 package onion soup mix, dry
8 ounces orange marmalade

Mix salad dressing, onion soup mix and marmalade together in a medium size bowl. Pour mixture over chicken, which has been placed in a rectangular baking dish that has been lined with aluminum foil or sprayed with non-stick cooking spray. Bake, uncovered, at 350° for 45 to 60 minutes (turn chicken breasts every 20 minutes, if needed to prevent drying out). Makes 4 to 5 servings with white rice as an accompaniment.

This recipe comes from the kitchen of the late Gene Belles, Chicago, Illinois.

Chapter Five

"Voila!" Dinners in a Snap!

Pattie Walker and Brenda Alonzo are moms with full-to-the-brim schedules who were the inspiration for this chapter.

"I have 3 little ones, and once I get home from week-night games or practices, I'm exhausted. We have breakfast for dinner far too often!" Brenda confessed to me.

"It would make our lives run so much smoother if you could put some easy-to-prepare, nutritious survival recipes in your column." Pattie requested.

The next day I began designing, "Voila!" Dinners in a Snap! a column that would appear seasonally, featuring an easy to prepare entrée, salad, and dessert; and garnished with a website and a cookbook suggestion to help streamline anyone's busy schedule. I was gratified in knowing this collection of recipes would assist super moms and dads in their efforts to serve their families' delicious and satisfying meals that would disappear in a snap!

Along with gathering a treasury of pinched-for-time recipes, I also began assembling a gallery of sports stories, which has brought me great sentimental pleasure.

This chapter begins with Speedy Spaghetti, Romaine Bread Salad and Applesauce Cupcakes, and a story about those frenzied days of quickly wearing out tires and crock-pots. It ends with making "Shaggy Dogs" and recounting our granddaughter's weeklong visit that made us thankful we had our children when we were young!

CB

On Your Marks, Get Set, Cook!

Driving by a playing field the other day and hearing the spirited cheers of parents immediately turned my thoughts back to the times when, I, too, was one of those enthusiastic parents who shouted encouraging words from the chalk line.

It was November 1976, and my son, Brian, who was 7, was playing in his third year of organized soccer. The Pacific Northwest was experiencing an unseasonably cold autumn and I vividly recall vowing, "I will not spend one more minute shivering on the sidelines!"

For my pre-game warm-up, before the Saturday game, I started my layering with a pair of long wool underwear. Next, I donned a bulky fisherman's knit sweater along with my heaviest long pants, topped with my down-filled, ankle length winter coat. To this arctic ensemble I added a wool watch cap, wool gloves, wool sox and my insulated Moon boots. I couldn't have been cozier! And, I was confident that my teeth would not be chattering before the first foul was called.

Long before half-time my face began to flush - I removed my knit cap. "Do you suppose I've over-dressed for this occasion?" I commented to my daughter, who at 9 seemed oblivious to the weather, even with her maraschino red button nose.

Soon I began to perspire as though I was in the full bloom of summer heat and before long my whole body was enveloped in an unrelenting hot flash. I took off my coat, which gave me momentary relief, but I was too late. Perspiration droplets had begun absorbing into my wool garments - I started itching!

I pondered my options.

My sweater and pants were the next items of clothing that would need to be removed; however, shedding them would reveal my long johns. "I'm going to the car to take off my long underwear," I whispered to my daughter.

Soccer players, and what seemed like a multitude of sports enthusiasts, were streaming past the station wagon as if they didn't have a play-off game to watch. I remember being thankful for my flexibility as I removed the long underwear in the front seat of our 9-passenger, 9-window, four-wheeled fishbowl.

Later that evening, while I surveyed the pantry deciding what to whip up for dinner, my family recounted the events of the game. They agreed that I'd earned my stripes after changing my clothes in the front seat of the car rather than miss a spectacular play or an outstanding goal. I earned the title of Devoted Soccer Mom!

Today's column is for those parents who spend a good deal of their time ferrying children to after school activities and for those who don't have a lot of time to spend in the kitchen. The recipes I've chosen require on-hand ingredients and can be prepared in 30 minutes or less. I think keeping a well-stocked larder and refrigerator are key factors in preparing scrumptious express meals, which offer comfort at the end of one's turbulent day.

Speedy Spaghetti is a recipe that I discovered in a child's cookbook. I found it to be so tasty and easy to prepare that I've been making it whenever I'm pressed for time and my appetite screams for spaghetti with red sauce.

Romaine Bread Salad is a breeze to assemble, and it conveniently combines salad and bread, which are two winning compliments to a spaghetti dinner. I've just recently added this unique and flavorful Italian bread salad to my Speedy and Savory recipe file.

And, what kid of any age doesn't like applesauce or peanut butter? My standby recipe for Applesauce Cupcakes with Peanut Butter Frosting utilizes basic pantry stock ingredients to create an all-time family favorite! These moist cupcakes are a terrific year round treat with the popular combination of cinnamon and apples, topped with sweetened peanut butter frosting.

Fall is the time of year when Jack Frost is peeking at us from around every corner and many parents are cheering and shivering on the sidelines. However, I think these quick-to-fix recipes will earn you a warm, "RAH, RAH, RAH" at the dinner table.

Speedy Spaghetti

1 pound lean ground beef
2¾ cups water
1 -15 ounce can tomato sauce
1 tablespoon dried minced onion
1 teaspoon dried oregano, crushed
½ teaspoon dried basil, crushed
¼ teaspoon salt
¼ teaspoon garlic powder
¼ teaspoon ground black pepper
6 ounces thin spaghetti
¼ to ½ cup grated Parmesan cheese

Brown ground beef in a large skillet over medium-high heat, breaking it into pieces as it cooks. When meat is brown, drain off excess fat.

Stir in water, tomato sauce, onion, oregano, basil, salt garlic powder and pepper into the pan with the meat. Cover the pan and turn the burner to medium-high. When the mixture begins to boil, break the spaghetti in half and add to saucepan. **Immediately turn the burner to low heat.** Place the lid on the pan and simmer for 30 to 40 minutes, stirring frequently. Sprinkle with Parmesan cheese, if desired. Makes 4 servings.

Romaine Bread Salad

8 ounces day-old Italian bread, torn into chunks
3 cups ripe tomatoes cut into chunks
¾ cup red onion rings, cut in half and sliced thin
½ cup Parmesan cheese, shredded
⅓ cup pitted ripe olives, cut in half lengthwise
¾ cup artichoke hearts, drained and sliced (optional)
3 cups romaine lettuce cut into bite-size pieces
¾ cup Italian dressing

Toss bread, tomato chunks, onions, cheese, olives, artichokes and lettuce together in a large salad bowl, drizzle with Italian dressing and toss thoroughly. Serve immediately. Makes 6 to 8 servings.

Applesauce Cupcakes with Peanut Butter Frosting

½ cup margarine, softened
1½ cups granulated sugar
2 to 4 tablespoons powdered cocoa
2 eggs
2¼ cups all-purpose flour, un-sifted
1 teaspoon salt
½ teaspoon ground cinnamon
1½ teaspoons baking soda
¼ teaspoon ground nutmeg
1¼ cups unsweetened applesauce
1 cup nuts, chopped fine

Preheat oven to 375°. Using an electric hand mixer, cream margarine, sugar and cocoa together in a large mixing bowl. Add eggs and beat for 1 minute. Add salt, cinnamon, baking soda, nutmeg, flour and applesauce, beat for approximately 2 minutes, or until ingredients are well blended. Stir in chopped nuts (peanuts are best). Fill cupcake papers ¾ full and bake for

20 to 25 minutes. When cupcakes are cool, frost with Peanut Butter Frosting. Makes 14 cupcakes.

Peanut Butter Frosting

½ cup chunky peanut butter
½ cup margarine, softened
1 cup confectioners' sugar

Blend ingredients in a medium-sized mixing bowl until smooth and creamy. Makes frosting for 14 cupcakes or to cover an 11" x 13" sheet cake.

Website suggestion: www.busycooks.about.com
Cookbook suggestion: *Desperation Dinners*, authors: Beverly Mills and Alicia Ross, ISBN 0-7611-0481-X, cost: $13.95

Cooking Secrets
for the Busy Mom

"Hey, Mom! What are we having for dinner tonight?" my 8 year-old son, Brian, yelled at the top of his lungs from the backseat of the station wagon. Although Brian and I were alone in the car he was still revved up from playing a soccer game his team had just won against their fiercest rivals.

While trying to keep both my sense of humor in tact and my eyes on the road, I calmly replied to Brian over my shoulder, "Just like magic...dinner will be ready the moment we walk in the door!"

The inviting aroma of Braised Beef Tips with Mushrooms met us at the door as we straggled in from the car. The secret magic trick that I pulled out of my top hat on a regular basis was the use of my crock-pot.

Dinner had been simmering on the counter since early that morning. The night before I took a few minutes to prepare the Cabbage Salad and put it in the refrigerator to marinate. The salad was always a hit, probably because its sweet-tart flavors had time to meld overnight. The kids helped me make No-Bake Rocky Road Cookies early Saturday morning after watching their favorite Quick Draw McGraw and Roadrunner cartoons. They had to be closely monitored otherwise the cookies disappeared so swiftly that there wouldn't be any left for the upcoming week.

I felt gratified in knowing a complete dinner awaited us after soccer. I smiled to myself thinking that putting a respectable dinner on the table during hectic sports weeknights was similar to performing magic tricks.

Who needed a magic wand to create a tasty meal when I had my crock-pot? With minimal planning I was able to attend weeknight soccer practices, weekend play-off games, some of which, stretched into February, and still prepare a square meal for my hungry family to sit down and enjoy together at the close of a busy day.

Whether it's soccer, baseball, football or simply a frenzied day, you too can pull a simple sleight of hand, "presto, changeo, abracadabra," and voila – serving your family savory, no fuss dinners will be yours, and that's not an illusion!

Braised Beef Tips with Mushrooms

1 - 4 ounce can sliced mushrooms
1½ pounds stew beef, cut into 1 inch cubes
1 clove garlic, minced
1 cup onions, sliced
2 tablespoons shortening
1 beef bouillon cube
½ cup water
1 - 8 ounce can tomato sauce
2 teaspoons sugar
2 teaspoons Worcestershire sauce
1 teaspoon dried basil
1 teaspoon dried oregano
¼ cup water
½ teaspoon salt
¼ teaspoon ground black pepper
1 -15 ounce can cut green beans, drained (optional)

Drain mushrooms; reserve liquid. Brown meat, garlic, onions and mushrooms in hot shortening, using a Dutch oven or heavy skillet. Crush bouillon cube between two spoons; add to meat with water, mushroom liquid and remaining ingredients; stir. Cover and bake at 300° for 3 hours or cook in crock pot on low setting for 6 to 8 hours. Add green beans just before serving. Serve over hot egg noodles, mashed potatoes, or rice. Makes 4 servings.

Cabbage Salad

1 head cabbage, finely shredded
OR 2 – 1 pound packages pre-shredded angel hair cabbage
¾ bottle Brianna's Home Style Rich Poppy Seed dressing

Place cabbage in large plastic bowl; pour salad dressing over cabbage (do not toss), seal tightly, refrigerate. Toss thoroughly just before serving. Makes 8 servings.

No-Bake Rocky Road Cookies

3 cups quick oatmeal, uncooked
½ cup nuts, coarsely chopped
½ cup cocoa
½ cup butter or margarine
½ cup undiluted canned milk
2 cups sugar
¼ teaspoon vanilla
2 cups bite-size marshmallows

Mix oatmeal and nuts in large bowl. Combine cocoa, butter, milk and sugar in large saucepan. Cook over medium heat stirring, constantly until mixture reaches boiling. Boil for 1 minute, stirring constantly. Remove from heat and add 1 cup marshmallows and vanilla. Stir until marshmallows melt. Pour over oatmeal mixture. Stir with a heavy-duty spoon or spatula until oatmeal and nuts are well coated. Drop on wax paper by spoonfuls, top each cookie with remaining marshmallows. Makes 2½ dozen cookies.

Recipe reprinted with written permission of *Favorite Recipes from Ruralite Readers*, submitted by Mrs. Patti A. Amlin

Website suggestion: www.quickneasyrecipes.com
Cookbook suggestion: *The 5 in 10 Cookbook, 5 Ingredients in 10 Minutes or Less*, author: Paula Hamilton, ISBN 0-688-11927-1, cost: $15.00

Easy to Make Recipes? No Sweat!

"Briggs...get out on the field and cover for Smith!" the coach yelled to 6-year-old Amy, who was sitting on the sideline daydreaming about kicking the ball with all her might and seeing it zip past the goalie and slide between the goal posts, "Yeah!" the Bomber's score!

This was the first year Amy had played an organized sport and she was wholeheartedly embracing soccer. She fancied the thought of sharing "war" stories with her 2 rough and tumble brothers, who were 5 and 7 years her senior, and who had been playing soccer, baseball and rugby for as long as she could remember.

Hearing her name, Amy snapped to attention and ran out on to the field. She was thinking, "It's my turn to shine! At last, I'll be basking in the glory of being a winner, and I'll feel the athletic rush that Brian and John have talked about so much!"

With her in the game she felt the Bombers were sure to be the winning team! She could hear her teammates chanting, "Amy, Amy, Amy," and she could see them toasting her with frosty mugs of root beer at Pizza Hut during their victory party.

Amy had been out on the field for mere minutes when "BAM!" a player from the opposing team slammed into her. She fell to the ground with a loud thud. The team's want-to-be star player was down with a wrenched ankle!

Amy limped to the sideline; her dad made her comfortable and elevated her foot. Although her injury looked minor, they iced her ankle as a precautionary measure. Another player from the bench quickly replaced her and everyone's attention was immediately focused toward the action out on the field.

It wasn't too long and Amy was walking up around the bleachers talking with cheering friends, parents, grandparents, and siblings – basically anyone attending the game that'd chat with her. She swung on the metal gate at the entrance to the field, and whirling a jump rope, which she was using as a lasso, she was attempting to rope the fence posts. Amy's parents and the coach conferred with her throughout the game to see if her ankle was feeling well enough to return to the field.

"Maybe I'll go back into the game later," Amy responded putting them off for reasons that were un-apparent to them.

Needless to say, Amy never made it back into the game that day. The team managed to win the game without her assistance, and afterwards, at Pizza Hut the coach asked Amy, "How's your ankle?"

"My ankle doesn't hurt! I was just pretending that it hurt so I didn't have to play," she replied.

"Amy, I'm surprised, you've turned out for all the practices and you were looking forward to your brother's attending your games," the coach said.

"I decided that I don't like playing soccer! You have to run...people kick at you...and you sweat! The sweat is the worst!" she said screwing up her face in utter disgust.

That was the first and last game of soccer Amy played. The ironic part of this story is that 8 years later when the petite and dainty Amy entered high school, she turned out for sports and, sweat and all, went on to be an all-state player in the game of the crooked stick, better known as lacrosse.

Although soccer has come to a close for this season, I believe basketball, wrestling and gymnastics are gearing up. Whatever activity your children are participating in, you won't have to work up a sweat in the kitchen when you try these recipes, which are quick and easy for busy parents to prepare and kids will say, "Hey, Mom, this is scrump-de-le-umptious!"

Mom's Sloppy Joes

1 pound lean ground beef
½ cup onion, chopped
2 cans Campbell's condensed Vegetarian Vegetable Soup
1 stick margarine or butter, softened
6 to 8 hamburger buns

Brown hamburger and onion together in a large skillet over medium heat; drain off any excess fat. Add soup and heat thoroughly. Butter hamburger buns and toast under broiler; top with sloppy Joe mixture; serve immediately. Makes 6 to 8 servings.

Patty's Citrus Salad

One package lettuce salad mix
1 small can mandarin oranges, partially drained
¼ cup white raisins
¼ cup dried cranberries
⅓ cup shelled sunflower seeds, roasted and salted
½ bottle Best Foods Asian Sesame or a citrus (orange) based salad dressing

Combine lettuce salad mix, mandarin oranges, raisins, cranberries, sunflower seeds and dressing. Mix for 2 minutes. Makes 8 side salads.

Recipe comes from the kitchen of Patty Johnson, Renton, Washington.

Note: Add 12 ounces grilled chicken breast to Patty's Citrus Salad to make 4 servings as a main dish salad. Mm, delicious! Your kids will want this for dinner every night!

Apple Crisp

4 cups sliced, pared, and cored baking apples
¾ cup brown sugar, packed
½ cup all purpose flour
½ cup rolled oats (old fashioned)
¾ teaspoon ground nutmeg
½ teaspoon ground cinnamon
⅓ cup butter or margarine, softened

Preheat oven to 375°. Spread sliced apples in the bottom of a greased 8" square pan. Combine sugar, flour, oats, nutmeg, and cinnamon; cut in butter until crumbly, sprinkle mixture over apples. Bake, uncovered, 30 to 35 minutes or until apples are tender and top is golden brown. Serve with fresh whipped cream or ice cream. Makes 6 servings.

Website suggestion: busycooks.com
Cookbook suggestion: *The Four Ingredient Cookbook*, authors Linda Coffee and Emily Cale, ISBN 0-9677932-4-6

Nothing Like a Grandchild to Keep us Young

"Grandma, print the recipes for Ice Cream Snowballs, Shaggy Dogs and Quickie Pizzas in the newspaper. Those are the recipes the kids liked most!" These were Arianna's parting words as she adjusted her shades and began boarding a Seattle bound airplane.

She waved goodbye to us with her free hand. Her other hand was occupied with a Fun Dip candy packet; her new ultra-cool fluorescent orange Power Puff Girls CD holder was dangling from her shoulder.

Our 8 year-old granddaughter, Arianna, was going home, having just spent 8 days with us. Prior to the young city girl's arrival, we planned activities that would keep her active during her first stay with Gramma Cindy and Grandpa Ed.

Her visit coincided with a cooking class I was teaching for New Mexico State University, called "For Kids Only", so we promptly enrolled her in the class. We knew that swimming would be a daily must and Arianna was especially excited about meeting, Leon, our dog who would captivate her with his bag of tricks, which consists mostly of his begging for treats.

Arianna was very enthusiastic about the cooking class. When I asked her, "Do you think the other kids liked the Cocoa Snowballs as much as you did?" She rolled her big brown eyes, licked her lips dramatically, and replied, "Slurp, slurp! They all luuuved them!" With her remarks, I knew the class was a hit!

Every day after class Arianna hinted that it was time to go swimming, "Gramma, I'm steaming hot!" she'd announce. She shook her head like a 1940s movie starlet and lifted her black hair off her shoulders, droplets of perspiration streamed down her back. So, after preparing a repeat of whatever we'd made in cooking class that day, we were off to take a long dip in the pool. The 45-degree temperature increase between Seattle and Carlsbad was melting our little water baby.

In our *spare* time we went to see the movie *Atlantis* where not only did I watch a Disney movie, which I hadn't done for at least 12 years, but I observed with amazement that Arianna nibbled away an entire box of pink sweet-tart candy *worms*.

Near the end of the week, we attended Ed's company picnic. Arianna careened through 10 kiddy carnival games before Ed and I had popped the tops from our sodas. This was the portion of Arianna's visit where we were introduced to Fun Dip candy, which in texture and color resembles turquoise colored sand. That evening we were charmed into eating Sonic burgers and fries for dinner.

Arianna made several new friends in our neighborhood. This led to an overnighter at Arianna's house. I learned that we have a LOT more children on our block than I would have ever dreamed possible and that Post actually manufactures a Rugrats cereal for kids.

My feet didn't stop throbbing for 3 days after Arianna stepped onto her homebound airplane. Leon, who incidentally had been renamed "Buddy" by Arianna, didn't lift his weary head off his pillow for 72 hours. Ed felt smug about still having energy left after Arianna's visit. Somehow, I think he'll be smiling on the other side of his face when he bolsters the courage to step onto the scales.

During Arianna's visit it occurred to me that children help us stay young. They keep us so busy that we don't have time to think about the golden years tapping us on the shoulder. And, bless their little hearts, they enhance our awareness of what's cool in the kid's food world.

Indeed, there's nothing like a grandchild to light up your life, wear you to a frazzle and lead you down a slippery slope to purchasing Funyum chips, Snicker's Ice Cream Bars and Atlantis cookies, along with motoring about town to frequent McDonald's, Baskin Robbins and Sonic Drive-ins.

Ice Cream Snowballs

½ cup chocolate-flavored crisp rice cereal
¼ cup coconut, flaked
¼ cup nuts, chopped
1 pint vanilla ice cream

Put the cereal, coconut and nuts in a medium-sized mixing bowl. Stir with a wooden spoon. Using an ice cream scoop or large spoon, scoop out 4 balls of ice cream. Drop each ball, one at a time, into the cereal mixture. Roll the ball around till it is coated. Work quickly so the ice cream doesn't melt. Place the ice cream balls on a baking sheet. Place them in the freezer for 15 minutes or till serving time. To serve, put each ice cream ball in a dessert dish or serve in ice cream cones. Makes 4 servings.

Shaggy Dogs, a.k.a. Bully Bulldogs, Mangy Mutts, and Springer Spaniels

1⅓ cups semi-sweet chocolate chips
1 to 2 teaspoons shortening (not butter, margarine, milk, cream or water)
30 large marshmallows
30 toothpicks
3 cups shredded coconut **OR** 2 cups chopped peanuts, **OR** 2 cups finely crushed graham cracker crumbs, **OR** chocolate or multi-colored sprinkles

Melt chips with shortening in top of double boiler over water or in microwave (chocolate burns very easily). Add more shortening if necessary to get a good dipping consistency. Remove melted chocolate from the heat; stir slightly. Place a toothpick in center of each marshmallow; dip each marshmallow into melted chocolate, covering completely. Roll in coconut; place on waxed paper, remove toothpicks and allow

Shaggy Dog to set-up 5 to 15 minutes before serving. Makes 30 dog-gone-good shaggy dogs.

"Rave Review" Quickie Pizzas

6 English muffins
1 -14 ounce jar Ragu Pizza Sauce
Topping suggestions:
1 cup Pepperoni, sliced thin
2 cups Mozzarella cheese, shredded
1 cup bulk sausage, cooked, drained and crumbled
1 cup fresh mushrooms, chopped
1 small can sliced olives, drained
½ cup green or red bell pepper, diced
1 small can diced green chiles, drained

Preheat oven to 400°. Split the English muffins; spread with 1 to 2 tablespoons pizza sauce; add toppings according to taste. Place pizzas on a lightly greased baking sheet and bake for 8 to 10 minutes.
Makes 12 individual sized mini-pizzas.

Chapter Six

There's Never Enough Dessert!

While reviewing the dessert recipes for *Pork Chops & Applesauce*, one sweet-loving connoisseur made an excellent point, "There's never enough dessert!" he cried. It was at that moment the title for the dessert chapter was born.

You'll enjoy eating your way through this chapter where you'll find recipes for a sinfully delicious chocolate caramel cake, a blueberry salad dessert that's so sweet and creamy you'll wonder why anyone ever called it salad and, for frozen confection lovers, a royal ice cream sundae.

The recipes are tucked between some of my most memorable stories and I've opened the chapter with one of my favorite misadventures, *Capers of the Apple Dumpling Gang*, and a recipe for Autumn Apple Dumplings ~ the queen of comfort food.

CB

Capers of the
Apple Dumpling Gang

The Apple Dumpling Gang was a comical western movie, with Don Knotts and Tim Conway, that I took my 2 mischievous youngsters to see back in 1977, and I believe the movie inspired the kids to pull an apple dumpling caper of their own.

I was giving a baby shower for a dear friend, April. I invited 40 women for a buffet luncheon, and because April enjoyed my "best apple pie west of the Cascade Mountains," we decided to serve individual apple pies for dessert.

A few days before the shower, my motherly instincts were aroused when my kids started making unsolicited dessert suggestions.

"Mom, I think you should make raspberry squares for April's baby shower," my son, Brian urged as he peered at me from across the table, slurping his way through a bowl of Cheerios. Typically he was a rough and tumble 10-year-old who expressed no interest in social events.

"Remember the mini-apple pies that we wrapped in foil last fall? The pies your sister and you carried out to the barn freezer for me? That's what I'm serving at April's shower," I reminded him.

"The little apple pies that we put out in the *barn* freezer?" It was odd that he needed clarification on which freezer.

"That's right." I replied.

"Oh, now I remember." He rolled his eyes upward looking thoughtful. "I think April would like raspberry squares better than apple pie, we use apples in everything!" Brian screwed his face up like he'd had one too many green apples. "Besides, Mom, raspberry bars have that sweet red stuff oozing out the sides. Mm." He smacked his lips convincingly.

"What's going on? Yesterday your sister said I should make lemon bars for April's shower," I asked trying to be casually unconcerned.

114

"Are you thinking of becoming a pastry chef?" I laughed and ran my fingers across the top of his sandy colored crew cut. "Get moving! I don't want you to miss your bus. And don't forget to get your frozen apple juice, out of the barn freezer, for your lunch box!"

"Hurry! Pick up your apple juice and catch your bus," I said to the kids every morning as part of the school day routine. That morning my intuition told me something was brewing and it wasn't apple cider! As soon as the bus dropped over the hill, I walked out to the barn for a peek into the freezer.

I was flabbergasted when I opened the freezer to find that all the mini-apple pies were gone. In disbelief, I rummaged frantically through the frozen packages.

My mind flashed back to the hours I spent in the kitchen every year during apple harvest. With 9 apple trees the entire house would fill with the fragrance of apple strudel, crisp and cobbler. I canned apple pie filling and preserved spiced apples. My golden, apple wine was an unusual wintertime treat. We pressed apple cider with our oak cider press and I dried apples for snack packs. We made our own apple sausage. In fact, we harvested so many apples that the pigs would merely sniff them and walk away – they'd even had their fill.

It was apparent that my children were full of apples, too! Because the individual apple pies I'd lovingly baked, gaily decorated and put into the freezer for safekeeping, had been pinched and tucked into the kid's lunch boxes to be enjoyed as their daily school desserts.

My panic started subsiding when I found a nearly forgotten recipe of my grandmother's for Autumn Apple Dumplings. The dumplings worked as an ideal replacement for the 40 miniature apple pies and thankfully, as time was of the essence, I discovered they were fairly easy to make.

Topped with real whipped cream, the old-fashioned desserts were a delightful hit at April's shower, and my *Apple Dumpling Gang* retired after learning that simply by asking, I could serve them plump fresh-baked apple dumplings faster than they could pull another infamous freezer caper!

Autumn Apple Dumplings

Syrup
1½ cups granulated sugar
1½ cups water
¼ teaspoon cardamom
¼ teaspoon cinnamon
¼ teaspoon nutmeg
10 drops red food coloring
3 tablespoons butter
Crust
2 cups all-purpose flour, sifted
2 teaspoons baking powder
1 teaspoon salt
⅔ cup margarine, softened
½ cup milk
6 medium baking apples (i.e., Macintosh, Granny
    Smith or Gala), pared, cored and sliced
Additional granulated sugar, cinnamon and margarine

Combine sugar, water, and spices; bring to a boil. Remove from heat; add food coloring and butter, set aside.

Sift together flour, baking powder and salt; add margarine and cut into flour until mixture resembles oatmeal. Add milk all at once and stir until flour is moistened.

Divide dough into 6 balls and set aside. On a lightly floured surface, roll one ball of dough into a 6" to 8" square and about the thickness of piecrust; place an apple in the center, sprinkle with additional sugar and cinnamon and dot with 1 teaspoon margarine. Fold crust around apple; pinch edges together, place in a greased 11" x 13" x 1½" glass baking dish with pinched edges down, and spaced about 1' apart.

Repeat process until all apples are wrapped in dough. Pour syrup over dumplings, sprinkle with granulated sugar, and bake at 375° for approximately 40 minutes, or until apples are tender.

Remove from the oven, cool slightly; serve warm with cream. Makes 6 generous servings.

Note: If the apple dumplings will be served after dinner, make half-dumplings by using ½ apple for each dumpling. The same amount of dough and syrup needs to be prepared. Roll dough into 6" x 12" rectangle and cut each rectangle in half to make a square then follow process the same as above. This makes 12 portions.

A Sundae Fit for Royalty

"*I scream! You scream!* We all scream for ice cream!" Dad chanted as we eagerly searched the grocery store aisles for the ice cream topping section.

He let go of my hand and reached for the chocolate fudge topping, "What do you think? Strawberry and maybe pineapple this time?" Jars of sweet syrups, tucked between his forearm and biceps, clicked together like pool balls being racked up.

"Pineapple. Oh, Daddy..." I rolled my eyes and added mischievously, "Let's not forget the bananas this time!" Giggles bubbled out of me. He frowned at me, pretending to be annoyed at the reminder of his famous faux pas forgetting to buy bananas for the banana splits we made at the family reunion picnic.

When we arrived home with overflowing brown paper grocery sacks, Mom would smile at Dad, as though he'd been naughty, and say, "For gosh sakes, Bob! Did you buy out the store? You even bought maraschino cherries!" Dad would wink at me. We all knew the cherries were the crowning touch. It was all devilishly fun.

A recent conversation with my mother revealed that Dad's love affair with ice cream started before I was a twinkle in his eye. In 1946 Dad was 19 years old and he'd just returned from serving in World War II. Shortly after he and Mom married, Dad went to work for Mayflower Dairy in Hermiston, Oregon. There he worked as the company's only ice cream maker, and it seems logical to us, that's when his passion for the sweet, frozen confection began.

"As a young man," Mom disclosed, "He went strictly for chocolate ice cream. Later he began to enhance plain vanilla with chocolate syrup poured over the top and a cherry as the crowning touch." She also reported, "He made the best ice cream that Mayflower Dairy ever produced and he brought surpluses of the stuff home in buckets!"

Creating mountainous banana splits in the center of the dining room table with Dad remains one of my most loved and vivid childhood memories. By the time my teens rolled around, I'd picked up Dad's frozen dessert habit. Whenever our sweet tooth danced a jig, which was almost daily in the summertime, we slipped away to indulge ourselves with a chocolate shake at Dairy Queen or to Baskin 31 Flavors Robbins for a banana split with all the trimmings!

In my early twenties I created the Royal Ice Cream Sundae for Dad on his birthday, which became his birthday cake tradition. Dad's been gone for over 10 years now, but this dessert is a dazzling presentation guaranteed to impress the most discriminating ice cream dessert connoisseur.

When I crown this magnificent mountain of ice cream and cream puffs with decadent toppings and maraschino cherries, I can see Dad sitting at the dining room table, winking at me with mischievous delight.

Royal Ice Cream Sundae

70 miniature cream puffs (see recipe below)
1 quart rocky road ice cream
1 quart vanilla ice cream
1 - 10 ounce jar chocolate ice cream topping, divided
1 - 10 ounce jar marshmallow cream

Prepare cream puffs and allow them to cool completely.

Remove ice cream from the freezer and leave at room temperature to soften for about 5 to 10 minutes.

Place a layer of cream puffs in an angel food cake pan with a removable bottom. Stir 1-quart ice cream to soften; spread over cream puffs in pan. Repeat with cream puffs and 2nd quart ice cream; finish with cream puffs. Cover and freeze for 8 hours.

Remove from freezer 15 minutes before serving. Turn out of pan by running a metal spatula around edges of pan; push bottom out of pan and turn onto waxed paper. Using large

119

spatulas, transfer ice cream dessert onto a cake plate (if necessary, return dessert to the freezer for 10 to15 minutes if it begins to thaw or drip). Drizzle with one half of the chocolate topping and decorate as desired.

For serving cut into slices placing a dollop of marshmallow crème on each piece. For the finale, drizzle 1 teaspoon chocolate (using remaining 5 ounces) over each slice. Makes 12 servings.

Note: This dessert is fail-proof as long as your guests like ice cream, and who doesn't? It's one of my favorite dinner party desserts because it can be prepared well in advance.

Variations: Be imaginative and use any ice cream combinations and toppings that sound appealing. For pure decadence, use coffee and chocolate ice creams with chocolate fudge and/or caramel toppings. Chocolate and strawberry ice creams with chocolate and strawberry toppings, sprinkled with coconut are fun, or use pistachio and vanilla almond ice creams with strawberry topping sprinkled with chopped almonds. Don't forget the maraschino cherries!

Miniature Cream Puffs

½ cup vegetable oil
1 cup water
½ teaspoon salt
1 cup flour, sifted
4 eggs

Heat oven to 425°. Boil water and add oil. Add salt and flour. Stir over medium heat until mixture forms a ball. Remove from heat and cool (uncovered) for 5 minutes. Add eggs, one at a time, beating thoroughly with each addition. Drop dough by rounded teaspoonfuls onto ungreased baking sheet. Bake about 25 minutes or until puffed, lightly brown and dry. Remove from baking sheet and cool. Makes about 70 puffs.

Timesaving note: substitute store bought whipped-cream filled cream puffs for homemade cream puffs. They can be found in the freezer section of most super markets.

Cynthia Briggs

Summer and Blueberries Go Hand-in-Hand

"*U-Pick Blueberries - 20¢ per pound.* This must be the place, but it doesn't look like a blueberry farm to me," I said to the kids as the car came to a stop in a gravel driveway that ended abruptly at the edge of a sprawling, overgrown blueberry patch. "There's no one tending the place."

The kids, who were 4 and 6, and I pulled out our shiny tin buckets and commenced picking the beautiful blue wonders. Some of the blueberry bushes were nearly 6 feet tall and as big around as my Volkswagen bug.

I wondered why no one manicured the fields and what seemed curious was the absence of an attendant to weigh the berries and collect their money. "Look at the ground between the bushes! This hasn't been weeded since God was a baby!" I sunk one foot into the cushioned layers of tall, bent-over dry grass. It felt much like an old, worn-out cotton mattress under my tennis shoes.

"EEK! RUN! THERE'S A SNAKE!" I screamed throwing my bucket of carefully chosen blueberries as I sprinted at breakneck speed to the car. Quickly jumping into the driver's seat of the car, I reached around to open the back doors so the kids could scramble to safety.

Once we returned home, Holly reminded me, "Mom, we didn't pay for the blueberries!" Collectively, the kids and I had brought home 1½ cups of inadvertently stolen blueberries.

In my terror, I had forgotten completely about finding someone to pay. "It's a travesty that whoever owns the blueberry farm doesn't keep it up better. All that grass, growing every which way – no wonder the field is snake infested! That was the fattest, longest, most intimidating garter snake I've ever seen! As far as I'm concerned our blueberry-picking days are over!" I raved.

At 6:30 the next morning I found a note propped up against the sugar canister on the kitchen counter. It was written in Holly's newly learned cursive: "Dear Mom, We are with Dad. We will be back by lunchtime. Love, Holly & Brian." I knew immediately that something was up!

While they were gone, I decided to surprise the kids by having their favorite blueberry treat ready for them to enjoy when they arrived home.

Sitting at the breakfast nook I wondered what kind of new adventures they'd have to tell me while they were gobbling down the cool and creamy Boo-Berry Salad.

Suddenly I was jarred from my thoughts when our 1950 Ford pickup truck came barreling up the driveway toward the house. A cloud of thick, gray dust billowed out from under Old Betsy's rusted frame. Betsy slowed down negotiating our circular drive and came to a clumsy, but momentary stop. I heard a weary moan as her gears reversed and she began backing up toward the raspberry canes.

As the dust cleared I got the surprise of my life - 4 huge blueberry bushes loomed into my view, sitting majestically in the back of dear old Betsy.

The kids talked their dad into taking them to the blueberry farm and paying for the stolen berries. While attempting to pay, they learned that the farmer was selling all of his blueberry bushes.

"Dad, can we *please* buy Mom some blueberry bushes? She says, 'our blueberry picking days are over' because 'where there's one snake there has to be a thousand'! If we don't buy blueberry bushes to plant at our house, we'll never get to eat blueberries again!" The kids seized the opportunity to ensure that we'd have fresh blueberries every summer.

Summertime Blueberry Salad

Prepare blueberry layer:
2 cups boiling water
2 - 3 ounce packages raspberry Jell-O

1 - 15 ounce can crushed pineapple, well drained
1 -15 ounce can blueberry pie filling
1½ cups fresh **OR** frozen blueberries

Using a large bowl, dissolve Jell-O in boiling water. Stir in pineapple, pie filling and frozen blueberries. Place in refrigerator for approximately 2 hours to congeal; stir every 15 minutes so fruit doesn't settle to the bottom of bowl. When mixture has thickened enough to support berries (do not allow mixture to fully set-up) fold into a 10" x 10" serving dish; refrigerate until set.

Prepare cream cheese layer:
8 ounces cream cheese, softened
1 cup sour cream
1 teaspoon vanilla
½ cup granulated sugar
½ to 1 cup pecans or walnuts, coarsely chopped

Cream together the cream cheese, sour cream, vanilla and sugar. Spread evenly over set Jell-O layer, sprinkle with chopped nuts. Cover and refrigerate for 2 hours. Cut into squares or spoon onto individual serving dishes. Garnish with big, plump blueberries, if desired. Makes 10 servings.

Note: Summertime Blueberry Salad can also be served as a light dessert, and it converts well when low fat, non-fat and sugar-free products are used.

This recipe comes from the kitchen of April Poirier, Auburn, Washington.

Blackberries Create a Love-Hate Relationship

Should we thank botanist, Luther Burbank for introducing the Himalayan Blackberry to the Pacific Northwest? The plump blackish-purple berry bursts with a distinctive flavor, which has afforded many of us with delicious pies, syrups and jams since the turn of the century. Personally, I'm thankful Mr. Burbank took on the task of identifying and propagating the prickly vines that originated from Europe, but some folks would choose to disagree.

This overbearing plant can make grown men shed tears of frustration. I've seen folks twist themselves in anguish because green thorny tentacles were spotted slithering over, under and through the backyard fence for the 15th year in a row. The hale and hardy thorny bush can cause neighbors, who once shared friendly progressive dinners, to feud like the Hatfields and the McCoys because of the out-of-control annoyance.

Growing up in the Puget Sound area meant picking blackberries with my friends during July and August. Armed with tin buckets and scrap lumber, we delighted in attacking the biggest and thorniest blackberry bramble we could find. We'd slide heavy boards as high as they'd reach onto a carefully chosen blackberry mound; then precariously walk up the plank, smash the wicked bushes down and fill our buckets with the choicest berries. We went home with battle scars on our limbs and reddish-blue stains on our lips and fingers. Our bounties were transformed into tasty treats that our mothers created in the kitchen. We never suspected that as adults many of us would be tempted to use dynamite to rid our gardens of the overly fertile plant.

Himalayan blackberries are responsible for one of the messiest kitchen disasters and, in the same year, the finest wine in our family's history. Unannounced guests rang the doorbell when my mother and grandmother, still in their nightclothes, were perilously moving a jelly bag of strained blackberries from the wine crock, in the dining room, to the kitchen sink for disposal. In their haste, and 10 paces short of the sink, the bulging cloth sack split wide open. Splat! Sweet purple mash unfurled across the white tile floor and decorated the oak cabinets with miniature blue-black droplets. They doubled-over with the giggles and weren't able to answer the door. It was a very good year!

Should we thank or curse Luther Burbank for his contribution to our lush green gardens and hillsides? I think most of us would agree that he did us a favor.

In spite of their dauntless proliferation, this native blackberry graces our taste buds with a unique and magnificent flavor. Granted, it's a love-hate relationship between Northwest residents and the Himalayan blackberry; however, love conquers in West Coast kitchens when bubbling, fragrant blackberry pies come out of the oven.

Just Plain Good Blackberry Pie

6 to 8 cups fresh blackberries, washed and drained
1 cup granulated sugar (less if berries are especially sweet)
1 teaspoon ground cinnamon
½ teaspoon ground cardamom (optional)
4 tablespoons flour
Dash of salt
2 to 3 tablespoons butter or margarine
1 teaspoon cinnamon **and** 2 teaspoons sugar mixed together (set aside)

Sift together sugar, cinnamon, cardamom, flour and salt. Sprinkle dry, sifted mixture onto blackberries. Mix gently, coating the berries. Pour berry filling into large pie pan that's been lined with (unbaked) piecrust (see Favorite Pie Crust recipe below) and dot filling with butter. Add top crust, cut a vent, and crimp crusts. Sprinkle finished top with reserved cinnamon and sugar mixture.

Cover the crimped edge with strips of aluminum foil to avoid burning. Bake at 450° for 10 minutes. Reduce heat to 350° and bake for 40 to 45 minutes longer or until bubbly in center. Remove aluminum foil strips 10 to 15 minutes before removing pie from the oven. Chill pie completely before cutting so individual pieces will retain a well-defined shape. Makes 6 to 8 servings.

Favorite Pie Crust

> 1½ cups flour
> ½ teaspoon salt
> ½ cup margarine, softened
> ¼ cup cold water

Sift salt and flour together into medium sized bowl. Mix margarine and sifted ingredients together, using a pastry blender until mixture resembles dry oatmeal. Add cold water and stir with a heavy-duty wooden spoon. Divide dough into two large balls. Roll out on a lightly floured board. Makes 9" double crust.

Hitting the Sweet Spot

"How long have you been playing golf?"
T.W. asked me when I called to make an appointment for my first golf lesson.

"I've never held a golf club or taken a swing at a golf ball in my life," I fibbed.

"That's okay! If you have clubs, bring 'em along with a good attitude, and we'll get ya started!" I liked the golf instructor's easy-going confidence!

The truth surrounding the fib I'd told T.W. was that I'd held a golf club on one occasion, when my husband showed me how to hold his prized number 5 wood, a Callaway Steelhead Plus.

"This is unequivocally the most unnatural position I've been twisted into and that includes my chiropractic adjustments," I told Ed, swinging and completely missing the ball.

"It takes a lot of practice," he replied with a wry smile.

"With some lessons I might be able to get my body into the proper position, but hitting the ball creates a whole new problem!" I swung at the ball, missed again and handed the club to Ed.

Two years had elapsed since Ed had purchased clubs for me, and during that time I'd allowed myself to feel intimidated by the fact that Ed had played golf for nearly 45 years. "Everyone was a beginner at one time!" Ed's words were always encouraging.

I really had no excuses for not learning how to play. I couldn't declare that the blustery Seattle rain kept me off the course. When we moved to Carlsbad, New Mexico, in June of 2000, the heat was entirely too oppressive and then, I think virtually overnight our summer rolled into winter leaving me without an autumn for golf lessons.

This year our fall has been balmy and beautiful, which means the time had come for me to put my pride aside and tee-off.

I snatched a few vintage golf balls from the bottom of Ed's golf bag, removed the manufacturer's plastic bubble wrap from my shiny new Wilson clubs, and took off for the country club.

My first lesson went well. I don't think T.W. suspected that I'd told him a mini-whopper about never holding a club. We got along famously.

"Pick up a club every day. That's the only way you're gonna learn," were T.W.'s parting words that day.

Heeding T.W.'s advice, every day between my first and second lessons, I blasted balls down the fairway at the driving range. By the end of my second lesson, visions of me exchanging high fives with female golf pros at the Dinah Shore Open swept before my eyes. However, my grandiose dream had quickly evaporated by the time I returned my empty bucket of balls to the pro shop.

It was difficult to walk a straight line. I'd developed, what Ed referred to as, PFM - his acronym for pulled fanny muscle, which I think he made up for my benefit. I learned later that following *too* far through with my swing is the main reason for developing PFM. I was experiencing a throbbing pain in my right shoulder, which led me to believe that every ligament attached to my shoulder joint was now permanently detached.

"Right shoulder pain is generally from repeatedly hitting the ground before you hit the golf ball," Ed told me ever so tactfully one evening when we were icing my shoulder.

It seems since my first two lessons I've suddenly thrown myself into planning our Thanksgiving and Christmas holidays. However, as soon as I can stop seeing the physical therapist for the tendonitis I've developed in my left arm triceps, I'll call T.W. and schedule my third lesson.

Golf is a challenging game; and it's far more fun than I'd actually anticipated, although there are days when it reminds me a lot of croquet. Much to my delight I'm beginning to fit-in with our circle of golf cronies. Hitting my first house with an out-of-control golf ball and losing a brand new Titleist ball in the Pecos River are, according to the local senior golf circuit, part of being indoctrinated into the game.

129

Learning some golf lingo has sped up my ability to play the game. For me, the words: fore, divot, hole-in-one and eagle, have all taken on a new meaning. With each round of golf, I'm missing the ball less, by executing more of what seasoned golfers call practice swings.

Hitting the sweet spot was a golfing term I found curiously perplexing. Then, one day I hit the ball with perfect form and seemingly everything fell into place. For the first time, charley horses didn't gallop across my abdomen and my PFM didn't bring me to my knees.

I felt the golf club connect with the ball at that perfect spot in the center of the club's face. I watched with exhilaration as my ball sailed down the middle of the fairway, landing amazingly close to the green. I recall hearing a crisp ping - the distinctive sound of hitting the sweet spot, which is sweet music to every golfer's ears!

Much like learning to play golf, my recipe for Hitting the Sweet Spot Cookies require time, patience and practice. As you carefully assemble, bake and dip these delicate chocolate covered, sugar cookie morsels, your reward will be a scrumptious maraschino cherry sweet spot!

Hitting the Sweet Spot Cookies

40 maraschino cherries, drained
¼ cup rum or brandy, optional
1 cup butter or margarine, softened
½ cup confectioners' sugar
1 teaspoon vanilla
2 cups flour, sifted

Soak cherries in brandy for 4 to 8 hours. Drain cherries and place on a paper towel to dry thoroughly. Preheat oven to 350°. In a large bowl cream together butter, powdered sugar and vanilla. Lightly spoon sifted flour into a measuring cup, stir into butter mixture. Wrap about 1 teaspoon dough around each cherry to cover completely. Place on a cookie sheet, bake 8 to 10 minutes or until lightly brown; cool.

Chocolate Coating

12 ounces semi-sweet chocolate chips (2 cups)
¼ pound paraffin

Combine chocolate chips with paraffin and melt in a double boiler. Using a toothpick, dip each cookie into the melted chocolate; place on a wire rack until chocolate has set. If desired, dip cookies a second time. Store in waxed paper-lined container, do not store in refrigerator; cookies do freeze well. Makes approximately 40 cookies.

Timesaving note: melt a 24-ounce package chocolate flavored almond bark; dip baked and cooled Sweet Spot cookies into chocolate; place on a wire rack until chocolate has set.

Shared Love of Oatmeal Cake Bonds Future Sister-in-laws

"So, do you like Teresa after meeting her for the first time?" Denise inquired during an early morning phone call.

I danced around her question, unsure as to why, but feeling reticent about revealing my answer. "She's a great cook – my brother is going to enjoy that! The oatmeal cake she brought was delicious."

I sensed Denise wanted more information, so I tried a waggish diversion. "She was kind enough not to remind me of another birthday by leaving the candles off the cake." My diversion failed.

Trying to recover, I trailed off the phone. "She's nice and she certainly loves my brother. I've never seen him so happy!"

My brother, Randy, who is nearing 46 years old, will be getting married for the first time in June. Teresa is a lovely woman and Randy has chosen quite suitably. She's friendly and cheerful, her smiles are generous and she laughs readily. What more could matter?

As I put the dining room back into order, it occurred to me that, yes, something else did matter. What I needed was a meaningful connection with my, soon to be, sister-in-law.

To partake in my birthday soiree, Teresa baked an old-fashioned oatmeal cake. Its 4 layers were slathered with rich, cream cheese frosting and it was elegantly presented on a metal pedestal cake plate with a puff of white paper doilies adorning its edges.

As I began tidying up the kitchen, I picked up Teresa's cake plate and carefully pulled the cake and limp doilies onto a utility plate. "That's a nice touch!" I thought. "Teresa put doilies underneath the cake. I guess I'm not the only one who still fusses with paper doilies."

I started to put the pedestal plate into the dishwasher. "Oops, the dishwasher may be too harsh." I feared it would get ruined.

I carefully examined the gray, somber pedestal. Is it worn silver plate, pewter or aluminum? There was no signature of origin on its underneath side. Esthetic beauty was absent.

However, beneath the plate's lackluster exterior it was vibrant with *life* marks. It gleaned shiny gouges, black smudge marks, sticky spots, and a few tiny cracks in the stem. The plate had priceless markings from escorting a countless number of cakes to birthday celebrations, anniversary parties and church socials.

I hand washed it in hot soapy water and buffed it dry with an embroidered cotton tea towel. Then I centered it on my antique dining room table, which was draped with a white, hand crocheted tablecloth. It looked beautiful!

When I returned to the kitchen, I felt my face soften with a knowing smile as I looked at the doilies for the last time before tossing them.

I picked up the phone and dialed Denise. "Yes, I like her!" I blurted into her ear.

"What made you decide so emphatically?" Denise laughed quizzically.

"It had to do with a pedestal cake plate and paper doilies!" I replied smiling.

Teresa's Oatmeal Cake

Mix together and let set for about 20 minutes:
    1 cup oatmeal (quick or old-fashioned)
    1½ cups boiling water

Cream together in a large mixing bowl:
    ½ cup shortening
    1 cup granulated sugar
    1 cup brown sugar, lightly packed
    2 eggs

Add oatmeal and water, beat for 2 minutes

> Sift together:
> 1½ cups flour
> ¼ teaspoon sea salt
> 1 teaspoon soda
> 1 teaspoon cinnamon

Add to oatmeal/sugar mixture and beat for about 3 minutes. Bake in two round cake pans at 350° for 25 to 30 minutes. Cool **thoroughly** on a cooling rack. To make four layers: cut both layers in half, length-wise using a long, sharp knife. Makes 10 to 12 servings.

Cream Cheese Frosting:
1 stick butter, softened
6 ounces cream cheese, softened
1 pound confectioners' sugar, sifted
1 teaspoon vanilla
1 tablespoon cream or milk

Mix butter, cream cheese and vanilla together with an electric mixer. Slowly add powdered sugar. Add cream and continue whipping with electric mixer for desired consistency (if needed, add more cream 1 teaspoon at a time).

Stack the layers with cut sides down frosting between layers as you go. Lastly, frost top and sides. This cake will have crumbs in the frosting but it adds to its homelike beauty. And, to me, it tastes better embellished with a paper doily and presented on a pretty cake plate.

The Cookie Monster
and His "Boy" Cookies

"*Gramma, you're gonna love* what's in this box!" Brian said to his grandmother with the most mischievous schoolboy grin I'd ever seen. The birthday package contained a large, brown, tree stump shaped cookie jar with a chubby squirrel atop, which served as a handle. The squirrel had an impish expression on its face as if to say, "I dare you to reach inside this cookie jar!"

"You have to keep it full of 'Boy' cookies!" Brian blurted out, startling everyone in the room. We all had a hearty laugh about Brian's stipulation on his grandmother's gift. That was the day we began dubbing Brian as our resident Cookie Monster.

Brian is 31 years old now with two little Cookie Monsters of his own who visit Great-Gramma's house. They face a devilish squirrel too because the squirrel cookie jar, which has been broken and repaired more times than I can count, still sits on Mom's kitchen counter – always full of tempting "Boy" cookies.

It didn't take too long for all cookies to become known in our family as "Boy" cookies because Brian's signature question was, "Mom, when are you going to bake 'Boy' cookies?"

"They're cooling in the kitchen," I'd reply. "You can have a few after you change your clothes." Then remembering that a few wasn't specific enough for Brian's cookie appetite, I'd add, "a few means three, Brian! And, the cookies have chocolate in them so don't share with your Irish setter pal."

Sometimes I'd bake cookies in the morning when Brian was at school and hide them in unlikely places about the house. Within moments of returning home, Brian could smell the slightest scent of sugar, flour, chocolate chips and nuts. He'd turn on his inner cookie detector and in 60 seconds or less, he knew the whereabouts of every full cookie tin within a three-acre radius.

135

Brian was a typical boy who attracted dirt like a magnet. He was always easy to find because he left a scattered trail of dirty clothes, school papers and muddy footprints. However, Brian was remarkably tidy and meticulous about covering his cookie crumb tracks.

Graham crackers were the only cookies I purchased from the grocery store. When homemade cookies weren't available to Brian, he was off to the kitchen, using the skill and dexterity of a CIA agent, to find the graham crackers. He would eat every cracker in the box and place the empty cellophane wrappers back inside the box. Then, with great precision, he'd re-seal the opened end of the box and place it back on the shelf as though it had never been touched. Amazingly, he never left a crumb of evidence at the scene of the crime.

To Brian, three squares meant cookies for dessert after every meal. He was busted more than once for eating the cookies out of his lunch box while he was waiting for the school bus. He couldn't resist an after breakfast treat with those sweet morsels rolling around in his lunch box just asking to be gobbled down.

It's been a lot of years since my kids were growing up, but sometimes I look back and wonder how many thousand dozen cookies I baked while they were school age. However, if the opportunity presented itself again, like every Mom on the planet, I'd preheat the oven and start baking my next thousand dozen "Boy" cookies!

"Boy" Cookies

1 cup shortening, softened
1 cup granulated sugar
1 cup brown sugar
2 eggs
1 teaspoon salt
1½ cups flour
1 teaspoon soda
1½ cups quick **OR** old-fashioned oatmeal, uncooked

1 cup rice (crisp) cereal
1 teaspoon vanilla
6 ounces chocolate chips
¾ cup nuts

Cream shortening and sugar together. Add eggs one at a time and blend well. Sift together dry ingredients and add to shortening/egg mixture. Add oatmeal; rice cereal, chocolate chips and nuts. Drop by spoonful on greased cookie sheet. Bake at 350° for about 12 to 14 minutes. Makes about 100 cookies.

Recipe reprinted with written permission of *Favorite Recipes from Ruralite Readers,* submitted by Mrs. Carl Painter, Nespelem, Washington, 1975. It originates from an old army cookbook.

"Boy" Gingersnap Cookies

1 teaspoon cinnamon
¾ cup oil
1 teaspoon ginger, ground
1½ cup granulated sugar (reserve ½ cup, set aside)
2 cups flour
1 egg
4 tablespoons molasses
2 teaspoons soda
½ teaspoon salt

Beat together cinnamon, oil, ginger, 1 cup sugar, flour and egg in a large mixing bowl; add molasses and beat well. Add soda and salt.

Form dough into 1½" balls; roll in reserved ½ cup sugar. Place on cookie sheet 3" apart. Bake at 350° for 15 minutes. Makes approximately 3 dozen cookies.

Thank you to the late Helen Robertson for this snappy recipe for "Boy" Gingersnap Cookies.

"Boy" Super Cookies
¾ cup granulated sugar
¾ cup brown sugar, packed
1 cup margarine, softened
2 eggs
1 teaspoon vanilla
1½ cup flour
1 teaspoon soda
1 teaspoon salt
1 cup nuts, chopped
2 cups quick **OR** old fashioned oatmeal, uncooked
12 ounces chocolate chips
1 cup granola
1 cup Cheerios
1 cup raisins, simmered in ¼ cup water for 5 minutes, if desired

Cream together sugars and margarine; add eggs and vanilla. Sift together flour, soda and salt; add to sugar/egg mixture and mix well. Stir in nuts, oatmeal, chocolate chips, granola, Cheerios and raisins.

Using an ice cream scoop, drop dough onto an ungreased cookie sheet. Bake at 350° for 15 to 17 minutes. Makes 4 to 5 dozen.

This recipe comes from the kitchen of Dick Body, Des Moines, Washington.

Heavenly Birthday Cake

When my party-loving friend, Denise, called and invited me out for dinner two days prior to my 50th birthday, I thought it odd that she didn't want to make plans with me on the big day. When we arrived at Anthony's Homeport Restaurant, I scanned the reception area looking for familiar faces, hoping to pickup signals if a party was in the making.

I sat down in the waiting area, sipping a glass of wine while Denise checked on the status of our reservation. I was still surveying the crowded room, when suddenly, as if he were sitting right next to me, I heard my son, Brian, say, "Hi, Mom, Happy Birthday!"

Immediately, goose bumps rose on my forearms and any thoughts of an impending surprise party vanished from my mind. Brian was out to sea on Navy business but his greeting sounded so close that I made another, more intense examination of everyone sitting nearby. Of course, Brian was nowhere to be seen.

"This is silly!" I said to myself. "Brian is attached to the *Kittyhawk* and he's out on maneuvers." A wave of melancholy washed over me. Tears welled in my eyes thinking about my 27 year-old son, now married, and a terrific father to his own little ones. Was it possible that so much time had passed since he was 10 years old, spending his afternoons jumping his bike over jury-rigged ramps in the cow pasture?

"Happy birthday, Mom!" I heard Brian clearly again. A single powerful throb stormed through my body, followed by an eerie chill.

My kids would be celebrating their 30th and 28th birthdays a few days after I turned 50. Knowing that the intuitive connection between parent and child can be amazingly keen, and knowing my senses were still so tuned in to my children even 10 years after they'd left home, I wondered to myself, was I psychically drawing Brian to my side to celebrate this landmark occasion?

139

My eyes began to spill over. I was searching my purse for a tissue as Denise returned from checking on our reservation.

"What's wrong?" She asked when she saw me dabbing at my eyes.

I handed Denise my empty wineglass, "I think I've had enough wine, I keep hearing Brian wish me a happy birthday!" I replied.

She gave me an understanding smile, "Our table is ready," she said, ushering me toward the stairs.

"Surprise! Happy birthday to you! Happy birthday to you! Happy birthday dear, Cindy! Happy birthday to you! And many more..." Combined with my emotional reaction to Brian's apparent telepathic birthday greeting and the surprise birthday party, I nearly collapsed.

With beaming faces and rousing voices, friends, family, co-workers, shirttail relatives, and I think, perhaps even a few people I may have casually met in the grocery store, were belting out the familiar birthday tune that I didn't want to hear on my, not so welcome, half-a-century birth year.

I'd no sooner sat down in the chair of honor than a firefighter entered the room who was decked out in bunker gear, and carrying what looked like a flaming, fully involved sheet cake. My heart sank. Surely, Denise wouldn't let anyone do this to me! I'd seen firefighters at other birthday shindigs and they...well, let's just say they entered the room dressed to put out a raging fire, but exited the room practically nude! Didn't she know this was not only in poor taste but that this kind of thing was downright EMBARRASSING!

The firefighter set the cake on the table in front of me so I could blow out the blazing 50 candles. A waitperson handed me a knife and the firefighter said, "It's time to cut the cake."

I thought it was awfully early to cut the cake, but I felt thankful that his clothes were still on his body and he hadn't started any dancing gyrations.

I could see the cake looked like my son's favorite, a gooey chocolate delight called, Heavenly Chocolate Cake. I felt, yet another tug on my heart, with an odd, hollowness filling my chest. "I hope Brian's okay," I thought. "He's so far away and anything can happen..."

Again, I heard Brian, "Mom, be sure to save me a piece of cake." This time he sounded very far away.

I felt frozen to my chair. Was I losing my mind? Or, was hearing voices another menopausal symptom? Whatever it was, dreading that the firefighter might be removing most of his clothing at any moment only added more terror to my already heightened emotional state.

I turned around to see at what stage of dress the firefighter was in. "I'll have some cake as soon as I can get this helmet off," he said. All my blood flowed to my feet. The man grabbed the bottom of the helmet and pulled it off his head.

"I've come a long way to enjoy a piece of my favorite cake and to surprise my favorite mom on her 50th birthday," Brian said with a peacock proud smile that boasted, "Did I pull this off or what?"

Heavenly Chocolate Cake

1 (2 layer size) box chocolate cake mix
1 - 14 ounce can sweetened condensed milk
1 - 12 ounce jar Smuckers caramel ice cream topping
1 - 8 ounce container Cool Whip, thawed
2 Heath or Skor candy bars, crushed
For best results, use the brand names suggested in the recipe and prepare the cake 1 day in advance.

Prepare the cake mix according to package directions and bake in an 11" x 13" rectangular cake pan. Cool completely. With the handle end of a wooden spoon, poke holes in cake. Pour sweetened condensed milk over top of cake, let soak in for 5 minutes. Pour caramel ice cream topping over cake, let soak in for 5 minutes.

Frost the cake with Cool Whip topping. Sprinkle crushed candy over top. Cover and chill overnight. Makes 16 servings.

This heavenly cake recipe comes from the kitchens of Mary Stone, Jared Collins, and Suzanne Creech, just to name a few.

Pooch Picks Pears and Pecans

We welcomed the pitter-patter of four little paws into our family when our neighbors had a one-year-old dachshund, which they were offering for adoption. It was love at first sight when we met Leon and we wondered how anyone could possibly let go of such a charming little wiener dog. We felt so lucky when Leon, complete with his leash and his security blanket, came home to live with us.

Now I'm the first one to admit that we dote over Leon. We think he is the cutest 22-pound doxie that's ever been born. We comment constantly on his playfulness and his cunning intellect. However, Ed and I have one unwavering house rule. Leon is not allowed to sleep in our bed – with or without us in it! We understand that Lele is a people pooch and likes to cuddle with us. And, trying to look at it from his perspective, the three big fluffy pillows on our king-size bed are almost too irresistible for any self-respecting canine to ignore. But darn it! Rules are rules!

Leisurely Sundays frequently get Leon into trouble. Observing Ed and me nestled against those tempting pillows reading the paper and watching television is more than he can endure. Before sunset, we find him snoozing like an angel on the center bed pillow. The expression in those sweet brown eyes say, "I know you love me and I deserve the same privileges as your grown up kids who are out of the nest. Move over, I'm gonna take a leap for the center pillow!"

Leon's previous owners knew their doggie well. They told us that pillows were fair game. We have come to understand the reality of those words. But to rephrase precisely, "Pillows, comforters, anything filled with batting are fair game!"

Turning a tiny pillow into a mountain of white fluff is an entertaining escapade for Leon and an obsessive malady that has followed him to our residence. He's amazing! He can literally fill his sleeping area, knee deep in pillow batting, in the

143

time it takes us to drive to the grocery store and back. And he can do the same thing the following day with a comforter.

Leon's former owners also mentioned that one of his favorite foods is pears, but nary a word about pecans. We started finding dozens of pecans, cracked, half-eaten, and scattered throughout the house. The guilty party became quickly apparent, as neither Ed nor I knew we had a pecan tree in the yard. We've offset his pecan-cracking craze with pig ears and rawhide bones.

We have more control over the pear situation because Leon's legs are too short to reach the countertop. But, come to think of it, the other day I noticed an extension ladder leaning up against the dining room table and…Ed was away at work.

Our sweet, people-pleasing badger hound is a loyal buddy in every sense of the word. When I ask, "Honey, would you please come in the den and help me?" Ed and Leon come through the doorway at the same time.

For 25 years I've been making this unusual recipe for Pear Pie with Crunchy Pecan Crust. With pears ripening in the crispness of autumn and pecans falling to the ground, I've come to realize that the unique combination of pears and pecans has added an interesting twist to our bond with Leon. Without doubt, he's captured a soft place in our hearts although he hasn't captured a soft place on our bed.

Pear Pie with Crunchy Pecan Crust

¾ cup pecans, chopped
6 cups Bartlett pears, peeled and sliced
⅓ cup granulated sugar
¾ cup flour
½ cup brown sugar
1 teaspoon cinnamon
6 tablespoons butter, softened
6 pecan halves (optional)

Make a single pie crust for the bottom of a 9" pie pan (see recipe below). Roll out dough and place in pie pan; pierce the crust with a fork and crimp edges. Sprinkle ¼ cup pecans into bottom of pastry. Gently press pecans into dough.

Preheat oven to 375°. Fill the crust with the pears. Combine the granulated sugar and 2 tablespoons flour; sprinkle onto pears. In another bowl combine remaining flour and pecans, brown sugar and cinnamon. Add remaining 4 tablespoons butter to flour/pecan mixture and crumble together. Sprinkle on top of pie. Dot with remaining 2 tablespoons butter. If desired, use pecan halves for decoration. Bake for 40 minutes. Makes 6 servings.

Basic Pie Crust – Makes 1 single crust

¾ cup flour
¼ teaspoon salt
¼ cup margarine or shortening, softened
⅛ cup cold water

Sift flour and salt onto softened shortening that's been placed in a large bowl. With a pastry blender, cut mixture together until it resembles oatmeal. Add water, all at once; and stir until mixture forms a ball. It's normal to have some unabsorbed flour left in the bottom of the bowl. For tender crust, do not add more water.

Tales of the Great Pecan Hunter

Dachshunds were originally trained in Europe for hunting badgers. I'm not sure why the Dachshund was chosen to hunt the nasty tempered badger, but I think being close to the ground must have been a definite advantage.

Fortunately, the dachshund has evolved into an affectionate, and sought after, loyal house pet. The fierce killer instinct has dissipated from the doxie breed, but I believe the hunter instinct remains because our dachshund, Leon, is formidable and dedicated when he commits to the task of hunting...pecans.

My husband and I are transplants from the Pacific Northwest and it wasn't until recently that we learned how prolific pecans are in the Southwest. In fact, we didn't know we had pecan trees in our yard until after Leon came to live with us, and mysteriously pecan shells began appearing in the living room, under the bed, crushed near Leon's doggie door and in every corner of the backyard and patio.

I'm proud of our native Southwesterner dog and he definitely earns his keep as our number one pecan hunter! He successfully finds the most elusive nuts that have fallen from the trees into the grass. He deserves much of the credit for our yearly storehouse of pecans, which is large enough to share with out-of-state friends and family.

Recently we took Leon to the veterinarian for a routine check-up. The vet looked Leon over and reported, "Leon is in excellent health, except I've discovered that he's gained 3 pounds in less than 6 months."

Ed and I looked at each other and laughed. "Having to watch our weight runs in the Briggs' family. Is Leon going to have to join us at Weight Watchers?" I asked.

The vet was clearly amused. He smiled and said, "Leon is going to have to cut back on his dessert and my educated guess is that he considers pecans dessert!" The vet patted

Leon's head and ran his hand across Leon's back, "Look at his coat. It's especially shiny, that's how I can tell you folks probably have pecan trees and Leon is getting fat from eating too many pecans!"

"Yes, we have pecan trees. In fact, Leon buries pecans in the backyard between the shrubs so he can go dig them up when he wants a treat. We didn't realize he's been eating enough to gain weight!" Ed replied.

On the veterinarian's advice we've started taking our little round pound, Leon for more walks, and we've replaced his pecan treats with low-fat alternatives, such as raw carrots and zucchini. However, at times it's challenging to beat the veteran hunter to the fallen pecans and we've started confiscating Leon's stash when we discover pecans that he's buried in the flowerbed or hidden under the blanket in his bed.

Under careful supervision, Leon still helps us gather pecans when I get the notion to bake a pecan dessert. So, when we sink our teeth into a luscious piece of the Best Pecan Pie in the Southwest or a melt-in-your-mouth Quick Crescent Pecan Pie Square, it only seems fair that we slip Leon a few sweet morsels as his reward for a hunt well done!

Best Pecan Pie in the Southwest

½ cup butter, melted
1 cup granulated sugar
1 cup light corn syrup
4 large eggs, slightly beaten
1 teaspoon vanilla
¼ teaspoon salt
1½ cup pecans, coarsely chopped **OR**
1⅓ cup pecan halves

Piecrust: prepare a single piecrust for one 9" pie. Filling: Combine melted butter, sugar, and corn syrup in a large mixing bowl. Stir in eggs, vanilla and salt. Add pecans; stir. Pour pecan pie filling into pie shell. Bake at 325° for 45 to 60 minutes. Makes 6 to 8 servings.

This recipe has been passed down through three generations and it comes from the kitchen of Tracy Cothern of Carlsbad, New Mexico.

Quick Crescent Pecan Pie Squares

1 - 8 ounce can refrigerator crescent rolls
1 egg, beaten
¾ cup pecans, coarsely chopped
½ cup granulated sugar
½ cup light corn syrup
1 tablespoon margarine, melted
1 teaspoon vanilla
Confectioners' sugar (optional)

Preheat oven to 375°. Lightly grease a 13"x 9" baking pan. Separate crescent dough into 2 large rectangles; press rectangles over bottom of pan and ½" up sides to form crust. Seal perforations; bake crust for 5 minutes.

Combine egg, pecans, sugar, corn syrup, margarine and vanilla in a medium sized bowl. Pour mixture over partially baked crust. Bake 18 minutes or until crust is golden brown. Cool; cut into squares. Dust lightly with confectioners' sugar. Makes about 2 dozen squares.

Spicy Pooch Adds New Flavor to Household

When Leon, our 2½ year old dachshund, came to live with us in August 2000, he brought his own unique kind of spice to our home. He's even gotten us interested in watching the dog shows on television, or maybe I should say, Leon watches the dog show and we watch Leon.

Like dog lovers around the world, Ed and I sat with Leon on the couch watching with eager anticipation as the 126th Westminster Kennel Club Dog Show judging officials chose a non-sporting miniature poodle, Spice Girl, as its best in show for 2002.

German shepards, schnauzers, Scottish terriers, collies, Brittany spaniels, every breed of dog paraded their form and fitness, as their handlers led them across the gymnasium floor. They were indeed, regal looking canines with well coifed coats, demonstrating their impeccable manners.

With each close up shot, Leon would literally fly from the couch and begin barking at the spotlighted dog and sniffing at the screen. When the dog show signed off for commercials or the camera was no longer focused on the dog, Leon would get a very quizzical look on his little brown face and friskily walk around to peek behind the television set, where to him, the dog had vanished. He'd sniff in the shadow behind the set as if to say, "Where'd he go? I know he's back here somewhere!"

When Leon couldn't locate the disappearing dog, he'd turn and look back at us with a hangdog expression that was enough to break the coldest heart.

Throughout the show, Leon made the same circular journey from the couch to the television set, barking appropriately at the show dog, sniffing the screen, investigating behind the set, sending another disappointed look in our direction, and then finally he'd jump back up onto the couch for the next round.

He was seemingly tireless in determination and tenacity to meet each dog, continuing on his quest throughout the entire dog show. Even when Leon saw Ed and me amused and snickering like two pranksters who had just pulled one over on the school bully, his spirit was surprisingly undaunted.

There were only a few deviations from Leon's sniffing out the competition routine. Occasionally, from under the coffee table, he'd posture a huffy growl toward the animated dog(s) who continually went on showing themselves to the crowd of hundreds, yet acted as though Leon didn't exist.

Far more interesting to us was how relatively disinterested Leon remained when the camera moved in for a close up of certain dogs such as a white bichon frise, or a brown and black Pekingese, as well as the newly crowned, queen of the dog world, Spice Girl.

In thinking about it afterwards, perhaps Leon didn't recognize some of the more exotic canines as dogs. The bichon frise may have looked much like the plush toys we've given him to play with and possibly the Pekingese appeared to be a small shag rug on the move. Even Spice Girl may not have resembled the kind of dog Leon's accustomed to seeing with black pompoms bobbling about her body.

While the three of us were taking in the dog show, we treated Leon to his favorite healthy treat of raw carrot sticks, which also served as a terrific distraction for his fruitless attempts at finding a living-breathing dog inside the television set.

During the commercial breaks, I whipped up my all-time-favorite carrot cake. Ed and I enjoyed it fresh baked and piled high with sweet and fluffy cream cheese frosting. "Mm good! How can something that tastes this wonderful be soooo good for our eyesight and soooo bad for our waistlines?" we exclaimed savoring every mouthwatering bite.

Did I feel guilty about giving Leon raw carrot sticks, while Ed and I devoured sinfully generous servings of moist carrot cake? Yes, guilty to the core! But, as far as we know, Leon can't read, so if you don't tell him, neither will we.

Carrot Pecan Spice Cake with Fluffy Cream Cheese Frosting

4 eggs
2 cups granulated sugar
1½ cups vegetable oil
2 cups flour
2 teaspoons soda
3 teaspoons ground pumpkin pie spice
1 teaspoon salt
3 cups finely grated raw carrots
1½ cups coconut, flaked
1½ cups pecans or walnuts, chopped

Preheat oven to 350°. In a large mixing bowl, cream together eggs and sugar until fluffy, continue beating with electric mixer, slowly adding oil. Sift together flour, soda, pumpkin pie spice and salt; add to egg/sugar/oil mixture and mix until well blended. Stir in carrots, coconut and walnuts; mix until thoroughly blended using a heavy spoon. Spray a 13" x 9" x 2" oblong baking pan with non-fat cooking spray and pour in cake batter. Bake for 35 to 45 minutes, or use the toothpick method to test for doneness. When cake is cool, frost with Fluffy Cream Cheese Frosting (recipe below). Makes 12 to 16 servings.

Fluffy Cream Cheese Frosting

½ cup butter or margarine, softened
8 ounces cream cheese, softened
1 teaspoon vanilla extract
1 pound confectioners' sugar, sifted

In a medium-sized mixing bowl, cream butter, cream cheese and vanilla together using an electric mixer. Gradually add confectioners' sugar, beating until frosting is light and creamy. Makes approximately 3 cups frosting.

Chapter Seven

Culinary Hearts

Doors to culinary hearts opened for me when we relocated from Seattle, Washington, to Carlsbad, New Mexico. The managing editor of the Carlsbad Current-Argus newspaper asked me to periodically interview and feature area cooks in my cooking column, which spirited me out into a new community meeting and mingling with kindred cooks.

From a writer's perspective, it was inspiring for me to hear how each kitchen-master attained his or her expertise. As I chatted with each cook, I began realizing that cooking reveals a map of our heritage, partnered with a way of sharing and giving of one's self. This helped to validate my belief that culinary hearts, wherever they beat, beat as one, and from all parts of this good old U.S.A.

This chapter is a virtual buffet of everyday chefs, most of whom stir-up their tantalizing dishes in the desert Southwest, but what's more meaningful for me is that their culinary hearts come from all walks of cooking experiences, creativity and lineage.

I think you'll delight in experimenting with interesting dishes such as Chef Tim's Chipotle corn chowder; Toni Torrez's fruit-filled empanadas; or Michael Johnson's southern-style T-bone steak, all scrumptious creations unveiled in the following pages, along with other hardy entrees, irresistible desserts and extraordinary salads – garnished with pictures of their creators!

Culinary Hearts is a chapter about you! Cooks like you from bustling cities to sleepy townships who need to keep the creative cooking juices flowing because, like me, you may find yourself peering down at a sink overflowing with New Mexico green chiles wondering, "What on earth will I ever do with all these chiles?"

CB

Green Chiles Galore

"What on earth will I ever do with all these chiles?" I asked myself peering into the kitchen sink filled to the brim with roasted, unpeeled green chiles. This was the first time I'd seen a freshly roasted chile, let alone face the task of peeling a half-bushel of them.

Fifteen pounds of roasted chiles found their way into my sink as a result of a tour I had taken earlier that day through Kathy and Gene Hood's 260-acre parcel of land.

Driving through the fields and over dusty rutted roads, the Hood's pick-up truck came to a bumpy stop. The sweet-smelling scent of freshly mown alfalfa spread through the air and chile plants blanketed the newly irrigated fields. Gene explained, "We grow three types of chiles: New Mexico 6 (mild), Big Jim (medium), and the small Barker (hot). I'd like to send New Mexico 6 green chiles home with you today." Gene's wide brimmed hat covered his eyes, but a broad smile revealed his earthy and genuine nature.

"A little mud on your shoes won't hurt this truck – it's for farming," Kathy motioned for me to stop trying to wipe my shoes clean. "To be a successful farmer, you have to love this way of life. The biggest plus is not punching a time clock. We keep our own schedule and have our freedom," Kathy said.

Gene told me that he has been a farmer all of his life. He tried working at the potash mine for a couple years but he said, "I couldn't wait to get back to the farm." Kathy is no stranger to farm life either. She was raised on a ranch, which was originally homesteaded by her parents in 1928.

"Mostly we grow chiles and alfalfa," Gene continued. "My dad bought this farm in 1947 and then I purchased it from him in 1976 when he retired. Over the years, we've tried a number of different crops, but 3 to 4 acres of chiles and 160 acres of alfalfa are the mainstay crops."

"Sometimes we feel like we're getting too old for farming," Kathy commented. "But we've decided to continue growing chiles for a while longer because the kids are starting to show an interest in farming. In fact, we couldn't manage without them!" Kathy beamed with the mere mention of the children. "During peak chile season, with the kids and grandkids pitching-in, we can pick and roast 40-50 bushels on a Saturday morning. It used to take all day to roast a bushel of chiles in the oven, but thanks to Gene, who built our roaster, it now takes just 3 minutes to roast a bushel."

Chiles are planted in early April and they're ready for picking about mid-August. They're on the vine for 30-40 days before they start turning red. "Our phone usually starts ringing in early July with inquiries about our chile harvest and with people placing advance orders. Depending on the weather, by late September we start getting into red chiles. We've had people out in the field on Christmas Eve picking red chiles!" Gene laughed heartily, clearly tickled by the memory.

I asked Gene and Kathy, "What's the most challenging part of selling chiles?" They both looked at each other and burst into laughter, almost like they knew I'd ask the question.

Kathy composed herself and said, "Trying to explain to someone over the phone how mild or how HOT our chiles are! Everyone's taste varies, plus the temperature of each chile changes from year to year. Gene has a chart in the barn that helps people determine which chile will suit their individual taste, but over the phone it can't be explained!"

By the time I finished mulling over my visit to the Hood's chile farm I had slipped the skin from the last roasted chile. The green mound of freezer-ready chiles seemed a wee bit intimidating to me.

But, Kathy's golden advice about green chiles saved me from shifting into panic mode, "You'll learn that chiles are standard fare around here and people use them in everything! Anything goes with chiles especially chiles rellenos."

Chiles Rellenos

4 large eggs or 1 cup whole egg product (such as, The Amazing Egg)
¼ teaspoon salt
4 teaspoons flour
4 tablespoons water
4 to 6 whole green chile (roasted, peeled, seeded)
4 to 6 sticks Monterey Jack or sharp Cheddar cheese (cut to fit inside chiles)
2 cups enchilada sauce
1 cup Mexican style cheese, shredded (usually Monterey Jack and Colby mixed)
¼ cup cilantro, chopped (optional)

In a medium-sized bowl, mix eggs, salt, flour and water together until light and fluffy (as if preparing scrambled eggs). Generously spray a 7" non-stick sauté pan with butter flavored cooking spray. Place over medium heat. Pour ¼ of the egg mixture into sauté pan to cover the bottom (like an Italian frittata or French crêpe). When the egg begins to set up, and brown around the edges, place a green chile that has been stuffed with a cheese stick, in the center. Loosen the egg from around the edge of pan and fold it over the stuffed chile (omelet-style or flip both sides to the center blanketing the chile). Carefully remove the chile relleno to a small oblong-baking dish. Repeat this process 4 to 6 times, until all chiles have been wrapped with egg.

Spoon enchilada sauce over chiles rellenos and sprinkle with shredded cheese. Bake in a 350° oven for 10 minutes or microwave on medium-high for 4-5 minutes until cheese melts. Garnish with cilantro, if desired. Serve immediately. Makes 2 to 3 servings.

Cynthia Briggs

The Party Girl Shares Grandmother's Cheesecake Recipe

Beverly Weston has a unique way of bringing pizzazz to the Community Service and Continuing Education programs at New Mexico State University at Carlsbad (NMSU-C).

"I enjoy people and entertaining, so it seemed like the natural thing to do when the staff at NMSU-C encouraged me to teach an Entertaining with Pizzazz class," Beverly explained. "I was flattered at their suggestion and decided, "Why not? It sounds fun!"

"My mother and grandmother had a natural flair for entertaining, which has influenced me throughout my life. They were meticulous about table settings and food served to invited guests was never less than perfect," she recalled.

Originally from Pennsylvania, Beverly and her husband, Bill, moved to Los Angeles, California, and then to Carlsbad in 1993, shortly thereafter, Beverly took a job at the NMSU-C.

With the onset of the 1994 holiday season Beverly suggested to her co-workers, "Let's make Christmas on the Pecos part of our campus Christmas party." Caught up in the excitement of throwing a party, Beverly quickly added, "After the boat tour, everyone is invited to my house for dessert and Christmas cheer!"

A yearly tradition was born and Beverly's co-workers have reaped the benefit of her gracious gesture every year since. She continues to hostess the campus Christmas party, which includes a Christmas on the Pecos boat tour followed with a festive get-together at her home. Beverly also volunteers her event planning talents by organizing the university's annual employee holiday party.

"Fun is the main goal for students who take my 2-hour pizzazz class," Beverly emphasized. "The keys to successful hosting are good planning and organization. It's rewarding to watch a student venture out into the role of Hostess-with-the-Mostess."

"For each Entertaining with Pizzazz class I prepare a main dish, several varieties of hors d'oeuvres and desserts for everyone to taste. I choose recipes that are tasty, of course, but I like to focus on foods that don't require last minute preparation so the hostess's time can be spent enjoying her guests. This is part of the planning that can ensure a smooth running event. I share all the recipes with my students and this year I'll have new ones to pass along. Think shrimp!"

I glanced around Beverly's office and jokingly asked, "Where do you hide your crown? Surely you've been crowned NMSU-C's Entertainment Queen!"

Clearly amused, Beverly laughed, "I've never been called a queen. However, I've been affectionately named 'The Party Girl' by my family in Pennsylvania because I always planned our family picnics, birthday parties and holiday celebrations."

She paused thoughtfully and added, "My paternal grandmother, who lived to be 95 years old, handed her passion for a lively party on to me, and I know she'd enjoy sharing her special cheesecake recipe that'll add pizzazz to any social get-together."

Grandmother's Cheese Cake

2 - 8 ounces packages Philadelphia Cream Cheese, softened
⅔ cup granulated sugar
3 eggs
2 teaspoons vanilla

Preheat oven to 350°. Cream the cream cheese and sugar together; add eggs and vanilla. Beat with a mixer until smooth. Pour into a small, greased spring form pan. Bake for 25 minutes. Cool for 20 minutes before adding topping. Reset oven at 400° to finish baking cheesecake with its topping.

Topping

8 ounces sour cream
2 tablespoons granulated sugar
1 teaspoon vanilla

In a small bowl blend sour cream, sugar and vanilla. After the cake has cooled for 20 minutes, pour sour cream mixture over the cheesecake. Spread evenly over the top and out to the edges of the pan. Bake for 10 minutes at 400°. Cool completely and place in refrigerator until ready to serve. Makes 8 servings.

Optional: fresh or frozen strawberries, raspberries or blueberries served on the side.

Local Man Makes his Living in the Meat Business

"*Something just drew me* to the meat cutting profession," explained Bob Dugas, owner of Lakeside Meats in Carlsbad, New Mexico. "I was a hunter when I was a kid and we butchered our own game so I was exposed to butchering at an early age. When I was in high school I worked part-time at Food Jet, which at that time was called Quickie Mart. Some of the old guys in the butcher shop noticed that I had a knack for cutting meat and they agreed to train me every day until I graduated from high school. I've been a full-time meat-cutter ever since," Bob laughed, recalling the early days of his career.

Lakeside has 12 employees who are constantly busy behind the meat counter Monday through Saturday. Bob is a tall, confident man who embraces the challenge of successfully running a small business. He views the changes in the meat-cutting industry as positive. Lakeside sells a large percentage of their product to hospitals, restaurants and nursing homes, which puts them under stricter U.S. government inspection regulations. Two hours out of every workday are used for documenting federal procedures, testing products, and monitoring and controlling refrigeration.

Bob sat down on a nearby counter stool and began explaining the meat cutting business, "The meat cutting industry has changed dramatically in the past 25 years. New sanitation laws and workmen's compensation rules have gained a fresh momentum in an effort to protect consumers and employees.

"In general, the new laws are good for all of us as consumers. But, I think the public may buy meat from a larger chain store with the misconception that the large outfits will have better, higher quality, and more sanitary meat than the smaller operations.

"All meat markets are under the same umbrella of U.S. government regulations, but the small markets are physically inspected more often than the big markets. Small outfits can offer safer meat with a custom touch and the only drawback may be that the price is a bit higher. Increasingly strict government regulations and inspections are causing Mom and Pop operations, such as Lakeside, to become extinct like the dinosaurs. It's really tough for a small outfit to stay in business when it's up against the big guy whose inspections are less frequent."

Bob continued explaining, "Purchasing meat from a custom market like Lakeside has its advantages. Number one, of course, is the constant monitoring and inspections of the meat to keep it safe for the consumer. But, what folks need to know about Lakeside is that we offer only Choice grade meat to our customers. These days there are only two grades of beef and pork available, Choice and Select. As far as I know, I'm the only store in Carlsbad that carries only Choice cuts in the meat case. Choice is more tender than Select and it's well marbled, with little fat on the outside, and the cost runs about 10% higher than Select. Unless it's marked otherwise, Select is what you get in the grocery store meat markets. Our Choice meats may be a few pennies more per pound, but you do, indeed, get what you pay for."

"Bob," I interjected, "from my personal experience, shopping at Lakeside is easier because I don't have any price vs. quality decisions to make. I can just pick out what I want, knowing automatically that I'm getting the lowest price on Choice meat.

"Something else I appreciate about Lakeside is being able to call you in the morning to place an order for a specific cut, and it'll be ready for pick up that afternoon. It makes me feel like I'm getting old fashioned, sawdust under my feet custom service coupled with the modern-day sanitation standards."

"That's what we like to hear from our customers," Bob said beaming.

Bob's response was quick when I asked, "What's the biggest mistake cooks make when cooking meat and how do we, as consumers, get our money's worth at the butcher shop?"

"The two common mistakes people make with meat are: they slice it incorrectly and they overcook it. The rule for slicing meat is to cut it against the grain. Often people will cut with the grain resulting in tough, stringy meat. If someone slices an inexpensive brisket with the grain, they'll be displeased with the result and probably never purchase it again; therefore, missing out on its low-priced advantage.

"The problem of overcooking meat speaks for itself," Bob continued. "A meat thermometer is the best kitchen tool anyone can own. By using a meat thermometer, meat can be cooked to the exact recommended doneness. Once it cooks past its proper temperature, it'll dry out and become tough. Those new fangled, electronic meat thermometers work great, but any type of good quality meat thermometer will do the job!"

"The best cut of meat for a person's dollar?" Bob rubbed his chin, contemplating his answer. "That depends. Meat prices fluctuate with the season – basically supply and demand will control prices. T-bone steak will be higher in the summer because folks are barbecuing, yet chuck roast will drop in price because it's not in demand. One simple way to save money on meat is to buy boneless cuts."

Bob reached over and handed me a yellow Post-It note. On it he'd hand-written his own special meat marinade recipe. "Oh good!" I said. "You remembered to give me a recipe!"

He gave me a satisfied grin and said, "This marinade recipe can be used on any cut of chicken, pork or beef. I use it mostly for chicken and beef kabobs. I think you'll like it. It's tangy and the lemon juice in it is a natural tenderizer, which will make the meat cook faster."

Bob glanced around his market with button-busting pride. Everything appeared to be running like clockwork. "I worked at Lakeside Meats for 25 years and then I purchased it 5 years ago when the previous owners passed away. Although cutting meat is a fiercely competitive business, I'm proud that we're

163

able to stay on top of the stringent federal regulations and continue offering fine quality Choice meat to our customers. I stay in the business because I enjoy serving people. That's what gives me joy in life!" Bob said, flashing a ready smile.

Bob Dugas's Kabob Marinade

½ cup cooking oil
⅓ cup soy sauce
¼ cup lemon juice
2 tablespoons dry mustard
2 tablespoons Worcestershire Sauce
1 clove garlic, chopped
1 teaspoon black pepper, ground
1½ teaspoons salt

Marinate (3/4" to 1" cubes) top sirloin or chicken breast for at least 24 hours. Place marinated cubes on skewers with your choice of vegetables (i.e., cherry tomatoes, bell peppers, mushrooms, pineapple chunks). Grill sirloin to medium (not well done), chicken or pork should be grilled until pink color is gone and juices run clear. If desired, serve kabobs on a bed of cooked rice.

Note: We tried Bob's Marinade on chicken and sirloin, and it's absolutely delicious! Way to go Bob...you know your marinades!

Creating Cooking Memories

"This Streetwalker's Stew recipe is what inspired me to create a memory recipe book," Suzanne Creech said as she gently ran her hand across the page. "A friend gave me the recipe when he first discovered the art of cooking. He took delight in exercising his new-found culinary creativity by giving a basic stew recipe a more colorful name," She laughed heartily. "It was fun watching a young person get excited about cooking."

Suzanne explained more to me about her hand-made recipe book over fresh-from-the-oven chocolate chip cookies and rich black coffee at her home in Roswell, New Mexico. "My recipes have become a part of me, so preserving the recipe in its original format is like protecting the relationship with a person that I hold dear, it's part of the bond I share with that person, along with the story behind the recipe."

Suzanne refilled my coffee cup and we continued our leisurely tour through her recipe collection that spans 30 plus years. "Many of my recipes are very special to me because they're handwritten, perhaps given to me to make for a memorable occasion, or exchanged under comical circumstances." She paused and said, "Every time I prepare a recipe that someone has given me, I take a mini-journey to visit either my sister, or my aunt, or whoever gave me the recipe. With my memory recipe book, I will continue making those trips and visits, but in a more organized way.

"I began my recipe book by first gathering up my disheveled, menagerie of recipes. Then, I placed them in one big pile next to a box of sheet protectors. My husband, Loran, volunteered to create a cover, which he did and appropriately titled it, *Suzie's Red Hot Recipes* with a ristra painted in watercolor. Didn't he do a terrific job?" She closed the book long enough to show off her hubby's fine artwork. "Then, my extended vacation down a very long memory lane began," she sighed and smiled proudly recalling her labor of love project.

From my perspective, Suzanne's memory recipe book is a culinary tribute to her life in the kitchen. It beautifully commemorates her mother, her sister, cousins, aunts, and friends, each one sharing a tasty sample of their cooking expertise and creativity with her. This is the reason that the book far surpasses being a recipe collection. The personal treasury with hand-written embellishments, such as, "Best Wishes" or "Good Luck" jotted in the margins, along with individual ingredient changes and serving suggestions sometimes elegantly noted, other times clumsily annotated depending on the author's style, maps the story of Suzanne's life.

"Each time I make a recipe that's written on personalized stationary, scrawled on the back of a crinkled deposit slip, scribbled on a dusty envelope or typed on a recipe card, I remember the person who gave it to me." Suzanne thumbed through the colorful, diverse book, pausing thoughtfully at several of the pages.

"See this little piece of folded pink paper," she held up what looked like a miniature origami. "I didn't know how to fold a burrito, so my friend, Sue Anne, in Missouri made me this tiny, paper burrito to demonstrate how to fold a burrito. I'll never part with this burrito as it symbolizes the caring connection I have with Sue Anne. It's the story behind the recipe!"

"Look, here's the recipe I'd like to share with your readers. I call it Lorelei's Chicken Rice Salad. My husband and I never get enough of it. It's unique combination of Italian seasoning and rice with crunchy pieces of almond and celery creates the kind of salad that we find is hard to stop eating once we start.

"The remarks that are scrawled all over the recipe show several of the roads it's traveled. What's funny, is that Lorelei made her changes to the recipe before she faxed it to me and two people previous to Lorelei crossed ingredients off and wrote their opinions and suggestions in the margins."

I was amused at Suzanne's animation as she recounted the roundabout route the recipe took before it found a home with her. "I can't help but wonder from where this recipe originated and how many stops it made that aren't noted!"

Suzanne chuckled playfully, "It appears this recipe's road trip hasn't come to a dead end yet and I'm really glad it, along with many others, took up residence in my memory recipe book!"

Lorelei's Chicken Rice Salad

2 - 6 ounce long grain and wild rice package mixes,
i.e., Rice-a-Roni (discard seasoning packets)
1 package (dry) Italian salad dressing mix
1 cup artichoke hearts, drained and sliced
2 cups celery, chopped
1 cup red or green pepper, chopped (optional)
1 pound fresh mushrooms, sliced
4 chicken breasts, cooked and diced
1 cup mayonnaise
½ cup fresh parsley, chopped
½ cup almonds, slivered
1 small jar pimentos, drained (optional)
1 small can sliced black olives, drained (optional)
Salt and fresh ground pepper to taste

Using ½ cup less water for each package, cook rice as directed (do not use seasoning packets). Mix Italian dressing according to package directions. Marinate artichokes, celery, green peppers, and mushrooms in prepared Italian dressing overnight. The next day combine rice, chicken, mayonnaise, parsley, almonds, pimentos and olives to marinated mixture. Add salt and pepper to taste. Chill and serve. Makes 8 servings.

A Taste of Italy
In New Mexico

L & M Pizza located in Carlsbad, New Mexico, offers a variety of pizza favorites that come bubbling from the oven with a distinctively spicy Italian flavor. Owners, Louise LaRue and Charlotte Miller, both New Mexico natives, opened L & M Pizza on August 5, 1998.

"Word-of-mouth is the best type of advertising for any business," Louise told me as she roasted green chiles on Charlotte's backyard barbecue. "It took about 8 months for L & M to get rolling. Before we knew what happened we got really busy and it's been that way ever since!"

"We aim to keep our customers happy, and we think that by making everything from scratch and using the freshest ingredients has a lot to do with our repeat business. For example, these chiles that we're roasting today will be peeled and put into our freezer to be used on our pizzas. They taste so much better than the canned ones," Charlotte said, bounding from the chair to help Louise turn the sizzling chiles.

Charlotte continued, "There are days when the business keeps us running for 12-14 hours. Louise makes all of our delicious pies; we bake the bread used for our sandwiches, and of course, the pizza dough must be ready to go! There's always something to do!"

Louise removed some of the roasted chiles from the flame and tossed them into a dishtowel-lined laundry basket before she turned the chile roasting operation over to Charlotte. "I think hard work and long hours keeps us out of trouble!" Louise commented, winking at Charlotte.

Stepping into the banter, Charlotte said, "Yes, we do stay busy – but nothing keeps us out of trouble!" The two women, Charlotte being Louise's niece, shared mutual chuckles. Their conversation revealed a warm and respectful relationship.

"We take pride in using our own recipes, particularly our recipe for pizza crust. We think the pre-formed crust, the kind used in most of the chain pizza restaurants, tastes about as good as it sounds.

"Our crust is light, and non-greasy, and our recipe doesn't call for cornmeal. Crust is everything when it comes to making delicious pizza. Our just right crust has a slightly sweet, yeast bread flavor with a delicate texture that melds perfectly with our fresh-made, spicy pizza sauce," Charlotte smacked her lips. "I like our crust so much that I could eat it baked with only pizza sauce on it!" she said brightly.

"We have great customers who have their particular favorites, but we'd like folks to know that we also offer a variety of delightful sandwiches, lasagna, spaghetti, chili, tacos, pies and cakes. One afternoon we started experimenting with our favorite ingredients and created our LL Special, the CM Deluxe, and the Mellow Yellow, which our customers enjoy," Charlotte said with a generous smile, boasting their accomplishments.

"We're not the only ones who work hard," Louise added. "We have 2 full-time employees, Jami VanWinkle and Amy Jaure, who work along side us every day. But, we laugh and have a lot of fun too – that keeps us going!"

Charlotte's face lit up as she told me about one of L & M's delivery goof-ups, "We're still chuckling about the time we were swamped at the restaurant and we needed to make a home delivery. The delivery person left in such a hurry that the pizza got left behind. She didn't realize the mistake until she reached in the back seat of the car for the pizza and discovered only 4 drinks! She made a swift run back to the store to retrieve the pizza! We're still ribbing her about the empty handed delivery."

Charlotte and Louise say the L & M Supreme is consistently their best selling pizza. Although specific ingredients for their pizza crust and sauces is kept in the family, they readily shared the individual toppings for their ever-popular Supreme: pizza sauce, Italian sausage, onions, pork sausage, pepperoni, mushrooms, olives, green chili and shredded cheese. Spread toppings, in the order given, over good quality pizza dough; then bake in a very hot oven.

"We like it when our customer's try to duplicate the Supreme but they invariably come back and say it didn't taste the same. It's possible that our special secret crust and pizza sauce recipes, combined with our super-hot ovens make the big difference," Charlotte explained with her eyes twinkling.

Perhaps you'll have good luck when you try to re-create the L & M Supreme. But, rest assured the friendly folks at L & M Pizza wouldn't let a fellow cook or baker go away without passing on a to-die-for recipe. Louise has graciously shared an antique recipe her grandmother Barthalamew brought to America from Germany in 1894.

Louise said, "We've always enjoyed Granny Cake with a cup of coffee, and warm from the oven slathered with plenty of real creamy butter. Others may prefer it topped with butter cream frosting making it more like a snack cake. Whatever way you prefer it with its old fashion blend of cinnamon, nutmeg and cloves we've found it impossible to keep the recipe a secret!"

Granny Cake

½ package dry yeast
2 cups lukewarm water
2 eggs
1 cup shortening, softened
2 cups granulated sugar
½ teaspoon salt
1 teaspoon soda
1 teaspoon ground cloves
1 teaspoon ground cinnamon
1 teaspoon ground nutmeg
3 cups all purpose flour
½ cup chopped pecans (optional)
1 cup raisins (optional)

Preheat oven to 350°. Combine yeast, water, eggs, shortening, sugar, salt and soda in large mixing bowl and mix well.

Sift together cloves, cinnamon, nutmeg and flour, add to yeast/water/egg mixture and beat well. Fold in nuts and raisins. Cake batter should be the consistency of thick pancake batter.

Pour batter into a 9" x 11" baking pan, which has been sprayed with non-stick cooking spray, bake for 1 hour. Makes 12 servings.

Kids Bake-up some Sweet Treats

"Mrs. Briggs…Mrs. Briggs!" An excited 4th grader squealed as she tugged at the hem of my blouse. "Did you taste the cupcakes - the ones with the white centers? I made them myself!" The youngster's sandy colored ponytails danced above her tiny shoulders and she kept grinning at me with eager anticipation as we walked toward the gymnasium.

"They looked too puffy when I took them out of the oven, so I s-q-u-i-s-h-e-d them down with my finger!" she explained, showing me her exact squishing technique.

"Yes, I tasted your cupcakes and they were delicious," I interjected, hoping that we were discussing the same cupcakes.

The results of Sunset Elementary School's 4th Annual Baking Contest had not been announced to the children. I realized the young girl's squished cupcakes had been chosen as one of the first place winners because she'd been instructed to gather in the gym for pictures.

My purpose at the school that day was to be one of 12 judges critiquing 2 divisions, each with 6 baking categories: breads, cakes, cookies/brownies, pies, best decorated and candy/miscellaneous.

"Do you mind judging the Bread category?" Shawna Mayo, organizer of the event, asked me upon my arrival. The inviting aroma of freshly baked chocolate brownies, piping hot cinnamon buns and breads stuffed with spicy cheeses engulfed the entire gymnasium.

"Mm, bread! It's my personal favorite!" I replied, glancing over the 4 entries I'd be judging.

I was pleasantly surprised to see that the baked products looked beautiful. The children's attention to detail and presentation was impressive, showing they'd taken their time preparing well thought-out entries.

One especially creative cake from the best-decorated category had an autumn theme with individual leaves decorated in orange, yellow and green, all arranged to appear as though they were falling onto grass. Most of the pie tops were adorned with decorative piecrust cutouts.

"Shawna, do the children make everything by themselves?" I asked.

"The kids do all the assembling and baking of their product with assistance from an older sibling or an adult," she explained.

"When you've chosen the first place bread, bring it to the front table, where all the judges will collectively determine the grand prize winners," Shawna said as she darted away to begin tallying the winners.

All the winners were appropriately awarded either a blue, red or white rosette ribbon. Prizes were boxed crayons for third place winners, a package of pencils for second place winners and first place winners were given a box of markers. In addition, the 2 grand prize winners (shown forefront in picture holding their entries) were each awarded backpacks donated by Athlete's Foot.

The school's baking contest held November 15, in conjunction with American Education Week, coincided with the school's annual fund-raising enchilada dinner and open house. The baked entries were sold at the close of the contest and all proceeds, including the money from the enchilada dinner, help to support parental involvement in American Education Week and the school's Parent Teacher Association.

After careful consideration and repeated nibbling of the scrumptious offerings, the 12 judges finally settled on Donnie Rodriguez's Creamy French Fudge and Ashley Pearce's Apple Pie as the grand prize winners. Donnie and Ashley were pleased to share their prize-winning recipes with us.

Create your own magic this holiday season by inviting your kids, your grandkids, or your neighbor's kids over to try these prize-winning recipes. You might be surprised to learn there's an aspiring young baker awaiting the opportunity to shine.

Creamy French Fudge
By Donnie Rodriguez

1 - 14 ounce can sweetened condensed milk
1 - 12 ounce package milk chocolate chips
3 ounces semi-sweet chocolate chips
1 teaspoon vanilla
1 cup pecans, chopped

Combine milk and chocolate chips in a 2-quart measuring cup or bowl. Microwave 3 minutes or until chips are melted, stir, add vanilla and nuts and pour into a greased 8" x 8" x 2" dish. Chill and cut into 1" squares. Makes 64 pieces.

Ashley's Apple Pie
By Ashley Pearce

2 cans apple pie filling
2 deep-dish pie shells (unbaked)
¼ cup brown sugar
3 tablespoons granulated sugar
2 teaspoons ground cinnamon
Dab of margarine
¼ cup milk
1 tablespoon granulated sugar

Preheat oven to 375°. Set one pie shell aside; roll out bottom pie crust and place in a 9" pie pan; using a fork, poke holes in shell; place in oven and bake for 8-10 minutes. In a large mixing bowl, combine apple pie filling, brown sugar, 3 tablespoons granulated sugar and cinnamon; stir well and pour mixture into pre-cooked piecrust. Put dabs of margarine around pie filling mixture. Roll out piecrust top on a floured surface. Use a small heart shaped cookie cutter to cut out four heart shapes, one on each quarter of pie shell. Place piecrust over pie filling; trim extra dough; pinch edges together in decorative manner. Rub a small amount of milk on the back of the small heart cutouts and place each heart decoratively on top of pie shell. Lightly brush milk across entire pie top and sprinkle with 1 tablespoon granulated sugar. Bake for 1 hour at 375°. Makes 6 servings.

Restaurant Spices up
Tradition with Technology

"Dora cooks it all!" is the promise Larez Mexican Food Restaurant makes to everyone.

"I do all the cooking. Anytime you poke your head into my kitchen, I'm here!" Dora Larez said proudly. "Sometimes I'm in the kitchen for 18 hours straight."

"I'm very particular about what we serve at Larez. Some of our customers have been coming into the restaurant since we moved here in 1971. They're very loyal, so in return I serve them nothing but the best," Dora said with conviction.

"For example," Dora continued. "I make everything fresh from scratch! We use only the best quality ingredients. One day we had to use a different brand of chicken breasts because our usual brand wasn't available. Well, it didn't go unnoticed; some of our customers sent their food back to the kitchen because it tasted out of the ordinary," Dora beamed. "That's how keen our customers are to the way we handle and prepare their food."

"I can't help Mom with the cooking," Kathy Larez told me. "She uses a handful of this, a pound of that and a pinch of something else. We've only been able to wrestle one of her recipes onto paper and that's Chile Verde con Carne (green chile with meat). It's the most popular entrée on our menu; it's been published in *A Taste of New Mexico* and it was posted on our web page when we initially went on-line. Our recipes remain a secret because they're filed in Mom's head!" Kathy laughed and glanced at her mother affectionately.

"It's surprising the number of people who don't know about us," Kathy looked perplexed. "Although, I think our website has given us a boost because we've received e-mails from people as far away as Alaska and Oklahoma."

Larez Mexican Food Restaurant has made its home in Carlsbad, New Mexico, for 32 years. In 1997, Dora and her daughter, Kathy, became a mother-daughter team in operating the restaurant. Dora continues with the hands-on cooking and Kathy handles sales and marketing. Kathy also oversees a website www.larez.net that will make your computer speakers' dance across the desktop to the tune of the *Mexican Hat Dance*.

"That computer stuff is what Kathy does!" Dora waved her hands in the air. "I don't know anything about it; my job is to cook and keep my customers happy. Our customers are very important to us and some have special dietary needs, so we use strictly Canola oil (except for the tamales, which have to be made with lard). I guarantee you'll never see a pool of grease surrounding your enchilada in my restaurant," Dora assured me.

"We try to be responsive when our customers have special needs," Kathy explained. "I worked with a dietitian to develop the *Larez Healthier Menu*, which is designed specifically for diabetics, heart patients and Weight-Watchers members. It offers plenty of tasty choices so folks with dietary restrictions can stay within their food program and still enjoy eating out. People just need to request the healthy menu."

Dora explained some changes that will be taking place in the restaurant this fall, "We value our customers and their suggestions, so we're honoring their requests by offering more fresh vegetables and homemade Mexican soup on the lunch buffet. We'll be moving the buffet table to a more convenient part of the restaurant. We've already added a fun Mexican fortune cookie, called a *Dichos* to compliment every meal – people love them!"

If you're seeking catering for a private party, a quiet dinner for two, a business lunch, or simply a healthy dinner, you can be sure that Larez will serve a remarkably delicious meal. There are two unique ingredients that spice-up Larez Mexican Food Restaurant – current technology and tradition!

Dora Larez's Chile Verde con Carne

(Green chile with meat)
1 large round steak or pork roast cut into bite size pieces
1 teaspoon Canola oil
½ large onion, diced
1 medium tomato, diced
4 long green chiles (roasted, peeled and diced)
Dash of garlic powder
Dash of salt
1 tablespoon flour
2-3 cups water

Heat Canola oil in large skillet, add pork and cook until medium browned. Add onion, tomato, chiles, garlic powder, salt, and flour. Cover, simmer over low heat for 15 minutes; stir occasionally. Add 1-2 cups water depending on desired thickness and simmer for 1-2 hours or cook in crock-pot on low for 6 hours. Serve as a main dish with beans and rice or rolled in a tortilla. Makes 4 servings.

Dora suggests, "Use all fresh vegetables when preparing this traditional green chile dish – you'll be glad you did!"

Collection is Reminder of Old-fashioned Cotton Aprons

"This red and white gingham apron with the chicken scratch embroidery is one of my favorites. I wore it last weekend when I baked fruitcake for my husband. It's fun to choose an apron from my collection and then head for the kitchen," Ada Kirmser said as she neatly draped her rescued aprons across the counter.

Ada and Lars Kirmser own and operate The Music Trader, located in Maple Valley, Washington. If you feel that you won't be making it to Washington State anytime soon, check out their website at musictrader@musictrader.com.

Between renting guitars and selling sheet music, Ada explained to me that in 8 years she has accumulated 200 vintage aprons. Her favorites are the 25-30, which have been hand crocheted sometime during the 1950s era. The remaining frocks are a parade of old-fashioned calico, checkered gingham, and airy voile fabrics. Some are trimmed in delicate white or ecru laces, while others boast a broad, bright-colored rickrack. The down-home fabrics and frills are reminiscent of the dependable aprons our mothers and grandmothers tied pertly around their waist and bosom.

"Each one is like my little buddy," Ada said, as she laid potholders across a countertop below a row of violins. She touched each potholder affectionately.

"Wait a minute!" I said laughing. "You collect potholders too?"

"Oh, yes. I've got 528 potholders which I've collected over the past 30 years," She said proudly. "Most of them are hand-crocheted – probably by ladies with napping children. Each one holds a special meaning; but I enjoy a bargain too!"

Ada continued, "The most I'll pay for an apron is $3.99. For a potholder I'll spend 50 cents. However, I paid $6 for this set of potholders because they're unusual and in perfect condition. That's the max I'll ever go!" She pointed to a set of muted purple, crocheted potholders that were artfully shaped into miniature Chinese pajamas.

"But my best, all around, bargain was this potholder set I picked up for 60 cents." She tenderly touched an intricately needled teapot and its matching sugar bowl.

"I feel like I haven't preserved the past if I don't buy a discarded potholder or apron that I stumble across in a thrift store or garage sale. They all need a home!" Ada said wistfully.

Ada's potholders were a pleasant reminder of the flower-faced potholders that decorated many kitchens back in the 1940s and 1950s. Do you remember the baby-doll potholders with brightly colored, billowy skirts? If my memory serves me correctly, our baby-dolls gazed at us from the kitchen stove back splash. And, it seemed to me that every kitchen had its share of hand-crocheted roses that covered shiny round metal trivets.

Seeing Ada's beautiful collection of aprons made me think of when my grandmother hugged me. My face always pressed against Grandma's fluffy lap, which was draped with a soft, well-worn calico apron. If she were making Blueberry Orange Bread, I'd invariably come away from the hug with my face and hair speckled with orange-rind batter and blueberries.

I rarely saw my grandma when she wasn't wearing a cotton apron. In fact, her printed kitchen pinafores were so much a part of her that I was in my teens before I realized that her aprons weren't permanently sewn onto her housedresses.

Thank you, Ada, for sharing your delightful collection of aprons and potholders. They stirred up a batch of sweet memories.

Grandma's Blueberry Orange Bread

¼ cup boiling water
2 tablespoons butter
½ cup orange juice
1 tablespoon orange peel, grated
1 egg
1 cup sugar
2 cups flour
¼ teaspoon soda
½ teaspoon sea salt
1 teaspoon baking powder
1 cup blueberries, frozen

Topping

2 tablespoons orange juice
2 teaspoons orange peel, grated
2 tablespoons honey, warmed

Melt butter in boiling water. Add ½ cup orange juice and 1 tablespoon orange peel. Set aside.

In a large mixing bowl beat egg with sugar until light and fluffy; stir in orange juice mixture. Sift dry ingredients together; slowly add to sugar and orange juice mixture. Beat until smooth (approximately 2-3 minutes).

Gently fold in blueberries (do not over stir) and pour into one large (or 2 small) greased and floured loaf pan(s).

Bake at 325° for about 70 minutes or until the edges begin to pull away from the inside of pan. Cool for 10 minutes. Turn loaf out onto a cooling rack and set upright.

Blend orange juice, orange peel and honey topping together in a small bowl and drizzle it over the bread while it's still warm.

When bread is cool enough to handle, slice into 12 to 15 slices.

Johnson Family Seeks Sauce of Life

My Daddy's Bar-B-Q was born out of a desire for owner, Michael Johnson, to spend more time with his family. Michael and his wife were tired of the corporate rat race and the district manager job that kept him on the road entirely too much. With the family in mind, they decided that Michael would make a major career change with the hope of enhancing their family's traditional values, even though it meant relocating themselves and their 4 children from Pennsylvania to Carlsbad.

Michael and his family arrived in Carlsbad in August 2000, and by November, colorful signs boasting My Daddy's Bar-B-Q started popping up around town.

"Carlsbad was our first and most logical choice for a second time around because during our visits with my two sisters, who live here, we observed the city's strong sense of community and emphasis on family life," Michael said, explaining his plan.

Michael continued in his South Carolina drawl, "My daddy ran a small southern barbecue catering service from his home, and I'm operating My Daddy's Bar-B-Q in much the same way as my daddy operated his business. However, I've added barbecue lunches and barbecue dinners, which I serve from a mobile unit that I can easily move to different parts of town.

"The curbside service worked out well until the weather turned cold, burr, burr, and that's when I decided it was time to move indoors." Michael laughed, hugging himself and shivering as though we were experiencing January temperatures.

"Conveniently, an ideal location became available just when we needed it. We had business phones installed, hung some bright colored flags on the front of the white stucco building and our base location was ready to go!" proud of his ingenuity, Michael flashed a broad grin in my direction.

"My daddy, Harvey Johnson, shared his original South Carolina recipes with me before he passed away 7 years ago, and he chose to give me his recipes because I expressed an interest in barbecuing and the catering business. But, neither of us ever dreamed that the recipes would be the founding mettle for my new career and such a blessing for my family and me."

Tipping backward in his metal 1950s retro chair, Michael related, "A result we were seeking through this lifestyle change was for my wife to become a stay-at-home Mom. When our youngest child became school age, my wife could join me working in our family business."

Michael is a family man with a plan. "My long-term goal is to expand My Daddy's Bar-B-Q to 7 southwestern locations; beginning with Artesia, and then on to Roswell, Hobbs, El Paso, and Albuquerque. However, before I start setting up shop in other cities, I want to make sure that I meet the needs of the Carlsbad community because they are the foundation of my success.

"We couldn't be happier here! And, I'd like to thank the people of Carlsbad for accepting me and supporting My Daddy's Bar-B-Q because it's through them that we have prospered." Michael's tone reflected his sincerity and gratitude as he said, "Customer service seems to be a thing of the past and we want to change that by offering down home southern hospitality to everyone."

Although the recipes used at My Daddy's Bar-B-Q are a carefully guarded family secret, Michael has graciously shared one of his personal favorites that he simply calls: Smothered T-Bone Steak. You'll find that Michael's unusual technique of marinating the T-bone at room temperature in a unique blend of spices and vegetables, and then grilling both over a low flame, is a melt-in-your-mouth combination that will make your taste buds sizzle!

Smothered T-Bone Steak

4 T-bone steaks
Garlic powder to taste
1 cup green bell pepper, chopped
1 cup Spanish onion, sliced
6 green onions, chopped
8 ounces Italian dressing
Black pepper, freshly ground

Place steaks in a large baking dish; sprinkle steaks with garlic powder, green peppers, Spanish onion, green onions, Italian dressing and black pepper. Cover steaks with plastic wrap and marinate at room temperature for 8-12 hours. Remove marinade with the onions and green peppers to a large piece of aluminum foil; seal edges tightly. Place steaks on a slow grill along with the foil wrapped marinade mixture. Grill until onions and green peppers are tender and steaks are cooked to desired doneness. Serve steaks with cooked marinade mixture as a condiment along with your favorite steak sauce. Makes 4 servings.

Michael wishes you, "Bon appetit!"

The Fruit Empanada Queen of the Southwest

"Your son tells me you're the fruit empanada queen of the Southwest," I said to Toni Torrez as we sat enjoying a cool drink in her cozy dining room.

"Oh, Ralph is always bragging on me!" Toni replied shyly glancing away.

"I make a lot of different desserts as well as birthday cakes and I even do some catering for small groups. But, empanadas seem to be my family's favorite. My mother taught me how to make empanadas when I was a young girl, which gives you an idea as to why I've become so proficient at making them.

"But what pleases me most is when the opportunity arises for me to inspire my 10 grandchildren to share with me the joy of cooking and baking.

"Three of my grandchildren have won top prizes from entering my recipes in their elementary school's annual bake-offs," I noticed Toni puffing with pride each time she spoke of her grandchildren.

Toni's granddaughter was a top-winner with her Old Fashion Bread Pudding recipe. The winning recipe was subsequently published in *Junior Chefs Recipe Cookbook*.

Being a top-notch baker isn't exclusive to the female side of the family. One grandson (Jesse Torrez, pictured in this chapter under Kids Bake-up some Sweet Treats) won first prize last fall in the Sunset Elementary bake-off when he entered Toni's Old Fashion Cookie recipe. Another grandson, who attends Joe Stanley Smith Elementary School, won second prize when he submitted Torrez's Peanut Butter & Cornflake Cookie recipe.

"The grandkids always want me to bake for them. At birthday time especially, they tell their parents, 'I don't want anything store-bought – I want Grandma to make empanadas for me!' "Her voice softened to even gentler tones when mentioning her grandchildren.

Clearly Toni is as intensely proud of her grandchildren's accomplishments as budding bakers as she is confidant about her talent as a dessert dynamo.

"I was born and raised on a farm in the Carlsbad area. My mother was an excellent cook and she taught me how to make everything!

"I was fortunate enough to be the youngest of 4 girls, so instead of working outside with the others I agreeably spent my weekday afternoons and weekends in the kitchen with my mother preparing meals for our family of 9."

When I asked Toni how many of these scrumptious fruit empanadas she's fried-up during her home-baking career, she thought for a moment, and then replied with a chuckle, "a whole bunch of them!"

I was delighted when she graciously agreed to share her family recipe for fruit empanadas. Toni's miniature, fried pies make a colorful presentation and they're packed full of sweet fruit flavors that say, "welcome springtime!"

Toni is creating a precious gift for herself and her family. She's bonding her family closer together by inviting her children and grandchildren to become an intrinsic part of her dessert-making legacy, which I believe contributes to her standing as the fruit empanada queen of the Southwest.

Grandma Toni's Fried Fruit Empanadas

4 cups all-purpose flour
1 teaspoon salt
1 teaspoon sugar
2 teaspoons baking powder
1 – 12 ounce can evaporated milk
2 eggs, beaten
⅔ cup shortening, melted
2 - 21 ounce cans apple, peach, blueberry or cherry
    pie filling

Glaze

½ cup confectioners' sugar
1 tablespoon butter, melted
1 tablespoon milk
½ teaspoon vanilla
Fruit pie filling

Combine flour, salt, sugar, baking powder, milk, eggs and shortening. Chill dough for 1½ hours. On a lightly floured board, roll dough until paper-thin, cut circles the size of a small tortilla, about 7½ inches in diameter.

Place ¼ cup fruit filling in the center of each circle and fold in half, flute edges and cut a vent; or roll up enchilada style. Fry empanadas in hot vegetable oil until lightly brown. Drain on a paper towel to remove excess oil.

While still hot, drizzle with prepared glaze and garnish with additional fruit filling. Makes 12 to 14 empanadas.

Mission Accomplished –
Not Just One, but Two Recipes
from a Professional Chef

"It's a good thing we like staying at The Lodge!" my husband, Ed, said peering through the lace curtains in our third floor room. "Cloudcroft is covered in a blanket of snow from the blizzard last night." Jumping out of bed I joined Ed at the window.

"Oh good! This gives me the opportunity to extend my interview with Chef Tim. Hopefully, I can persuade him to share his Basil Pecan Salad Dressing recipe." Ed and I both enjoyed the unusual dressing drizzled over our garden salads the previous evening while dining at Rebecca's Restaurant, which is located at The Lodge in popular Cloudcroft, New Mexico.

The anticipation of interviewing Executive Chef, Tim Wilkins, proved to be an energizing experience for me because Chef Tim creates all of the delicious menu items offered in the restaurant that operates within the walls of the majestic 100-year-old hotel.

A few hours later, Chef Tim walked up to my table in the restaurant and removed his towering white chef's hat. He nodded politely and sat down with a confidence that I liked.

"My husband and I have been staying at The Lodge for the past two days and now that it's almost time to leave we're snowed in!" I said to Tim smiling at the irony of the situation.

"Well, you couldn't be snow bound in a lovelier location. I happened upon The Lodge in 1983 and immediately fell in love with the area. I worked here for 7 years and then moved to Texas. In 1996 I seized the opportunity to return to Cloudcroft, and I've been here ever since," Chef Tim explained with a comfortable smile.

"We're impressed with the unique choices on Rebecca's menu that appeal to varied tastes."

"I don't do it all by myself. The staff functions like a closely-knit family here at Rebecca's so turnover is minimal and morale consistently remains high." He waved to a young woman driving out of the parking lot in a shiny black car. "She's really proud of her new car!" His eyes crinkled at the edges.

He cleared his throat, "Now, getting back to the menu. When we change the menu, not only the cooks, but also the general manager, and wait staff approves the new choices before any final decisions are made. The wait staff is proud of each new menu because their suggestions directly affect the customers in a very personal way."

Chef Tim reminisced about his life before The Lodge, "I was raised near Sacramento, California, and worked as a paint maker for about 10 years before I began cooking professionally. Although I'm of Irish descent, I grew up in the kitchens of our Italian neighbors and that's where my love of cooking was born.

"I learned early that customers want consistency and if the cooking staff is unhappy, often the food becomes very inconsistent. This sets the stage for trouble in the kitchen." He paused for a moment and said, "Something else I've learned is that mixing paint and cooking are similar - color, consistency, temperature are vital for success." He laughed heartily enjoying his analogy.

"Ed and I appreciate your flair for combining southwest cooking with traditional continental cuisine," I commented.

"I was a cook before I studied to become a certified chef so my approach toward cooking is probably more down-to-earth than a chef that's been through the war as they call it in Europe. The Lodge assisted me in becoming certified through a New Mexico Working Chef program. It's a terrific on-the-job-training program that enabled me to get my degree in three years." His enthusiasm for the program was evident and he highly recommended it for aspiring chefs.

"Learning new innovations to classical presentations never gets boring. Food combinations, preparations and presentations are forever changing. To me, cooking is an ongoing experiment and it's rewarding to learn what works best. A specific dish may have been prepared somewhere else, but adding your own touch makes it yours. It's very satisfying to me when I see people take pleasure in something I've created." He gave me a gentle, relaxed smile, and then he excused himself to begin dinner preparations.

As we drove away from The Lodge, I pulled a piece of white paper with notes and the recipe of Chef Tim's from my purse and proudly waved it for Ed to see.

"Did you accomplish your mission?" Ed inquired.

"Chef Tim has a refreshing, unpretentious attitude toward cooking. He was easy to interview. And," I smugly pointed to the typewriting on the paper, "getting one recipe from a chef is an achievement, but receiving two recipes from Chef Tim is a special gift."

The Lodge House Dressing - Basil Pecan Salad Dressing

½ cup Balsamic vinegar
2 cups olive oil
½ cup coarsely chopped fresh basil
1 tablespoon Dijon mustard
3 squirts Tabasco sauce
2 tablespoons granulated sugar
1 tablespoon salt
1 tablespoon black pepper, ground
1 cup heavy cream
⅓ cup chopped pecans
1 tablespoon honey

Mix all ingredients in a blender until coarsely blended. Chill; serve over green salad. Makes 1 quart.

Chef Tim's Roasted Corn & Chipotle Pepper Chowder

1 tablespoon garlic, chopped fine
¾ cup yellow onion, diced
1 cup canned **OR** frozen corn, drained and lightly roasted under a broiler
2 tablespoons Chipotle pepper, minced
2 cups cream **OR** milk
¾ cup celery, diced
1½ cups potatoes, peeled, cooked and chopped
1 quart chicken broth

Simmer garlic, onion, corn, Chipotle peppers, and celery in broth for about 10 minutes, or until celery and onions begin to soften. Add potatoes and allow to heat through. Remove from the burner and stir in cream. Serve piping hot! Makes 6 servings.

Note: Chef Tim's Roasted Corn & Chipotle Pepper Chowder is delicious and hearty, but it should come with a **WARNING LABEL** because Chipotle peppers are very, very hot! It's wise to begin with 1 level teaspoon of minced Chipotle pepper and add more (1 teaspoon at a time) to taste.

For more information about The Lodge and Rebecca's Restaurant at Cloudcroft, New Mexico, visit their website at <u>www.thelodgeresort.com</u>, "It's charmed."

Cynthia Briggs

About the Author

Cynthia Briggs has written a slice-of-life cookbook, which touches the heart of the reader as she journeys back to the easiness of simpler times growing up on an Oregon homestead, coupled with recounting the humorous misadventures of raising her children on a Pacific Northwest farm.

Cynthia's interviews with Southwest cooks highlight her ardent belief that through the joy of cooking ~ culinary hearts beat as one. She believes through the sharing of our recipes and food we engage in an ongoing connection with others, weaving unique bonds we carry with us through our lives.

Briggs makes her home in New Mexico where she writes a weekly cooking column, and teaches writing and cooking classes at New Mexico State University-Carlsbad.